CULTURE SMART!

ESTONIA

Clare Thomson

D1010280

·K·U·P·E·R·A·R·D·

First published in Great Britain 2007
by Kuperard, an imprint of Bravo Ltd
59 Hutton Grove, London N12 8DS
Tel: +44 (0) 20 8446 2440 Fax: +44 (0) 20 8446 2441
www.culturesmartguides.com
Inquiries: sales@kuperard.co.uk

Culture Smart! is a registered trademark of Bravo Ltd

Distributed in the United States and Canada
by Random House Distribution Services
1745 Broadway, New York, NY 10019
Tel: +1 (212) 572-2844 Fax: +1 (212) 572-4961
Inquiries: csorders@randomhouse.com

Copyright © 2007 Kuperard

Series Editor Geoffrey Chesler
Design Bobby Birchall

ISBN 978 1 85733 353 4

British Library Cataloguing in Publication Data
A CIP catalogue entry for this book is available from the
British Library

Printed in Malaysia

This book is available for special discounts for bulk purchases for
sales promotions or premiums. Special editions, including
personalized covers, excerpts of existing books, and corporate
imprints, can be created in large quantities for special needs.

For more information in the U.S.A. write to Special
Markets/Premium Sales, 1745 Broadway, MD 6–2, New York,
NY 10019 or e-mail specialmarkets@randomhouse.com.

In the United Kingdom contact Kuperard publishers at the
above address.

Cover image: Tallinn, Estonia. *Travel Ink/Robin McKelvie*
Images on pages 13, 31, 35, 107, 121, and 129 by permission of the Estonian
Tourist Board. Images on pages 114 © Larsz, and 145 © ikescs

CultureSmart!Consulting and **Culture Smart!** guides have both
contributed to and featured regularly in the weekly travel program
"Fast Track" on BBC World TV.

About the Author

CLARE THOMSON, born in London to an Estonian mother and a Scottish father, is a journalist, travel writer, and teacher. She read English at Jesus College, Cambridge. Her first book was *The Singing Revolution*, an eye-witness account of the collapse of Communism in the Baltic States. Clare has worked as a journalist and freelance writer in Brussels and London. She has written and collaborated on several guidebooks about Belgium and the Baltics, and contributed articles to British newspapers, including the *Times*, the *Independent*, and the *Sunday Times*. She and her family are regular visitors to Tallinn.

Other Countries in the Culture Smart! Series

Other titles are in preparation. For more information, contact: info@kuperard.co.uk

The publishers would like to thank **CultureSmart!**Consulting for its help in researching and developing the concept for this series.

CultureSmart!Consulting creates tailor-made seminars and consultancy programs to meet a wide range of corporate, public-sector, and individual needs. Whether delivering courses on multicultural team building in the U.S.A., preparing Chinese engineers for a posting in Europe, training call-center staff in India, or raising the awareness of police forces to the needs of diverse ethnic communities, we provide essential, practical, and powerful skills worldwide to an increasingly international workforce.

For details, visit www.culturesmartconsulting.com

contents

contents

Map of Estonia

introduction

For a nation of around 1.3 million inhabitants, Estonia has made a real impression on the world stage since regaining its independence less than two decades ago. In the mid-1980s, it was known, if at all, as a Soviet backwater, but the collapse of Communism saw the emergence of a republic determined to make up for lost time and establish itself as a forward-thinking Western state. The economy has been growing at a rate other nations can only observe with envy; the capital, Tallinn, has become a magnet for tourists and foreign investors alike; membership in the European Union and NATO has been achieved with ease; and Estonians have embraced the digital age with almost maniacal fervor.

At the same time, this is a nation distinct from its Baltic and Scandinavian cousins, with a language and culture very different from that of most European states. For all their love of Wi-Fi, entrepreneurship, and cell phones, Estonians are quiet and reserved, hardworking, fiercely jealous of their privacy, and lovers of nature. They can seem distant, almost rude on first meeting, but if you make the effort to get to know them, their sincerity and self-deprecating humor shine through. As one businessman who works in Tallinn observed, "an Estonian friend is a friend for life." Adding flavor is the country's substantial

Russian-speaking community, something of a world unto itself, but more gregarious and outgoing than the natives.

If Estonian reserve can be in part attributed to five decades of Soviet occupation, and the consequences of not keeping your counsel, other aspects of the national character derive from the many occupations Estonia has endured, and the locals' stubborn refusal to be subdued. Germans, Danes, Swedes, and Russians, both Tsarist and Soviet, have all had their turn at the reins over the centuries, and Tallinn's time as a Hansa port has left its mark. Yet traditions run deep in this forested, sparsely populated land, and in the folk-inflected music that has become one of its international calling cards.

Culture Smart! Estonia aims to help you navigate these swirling waters. It is for any visitor—whether businessperson, student, or tourist—who wants to understand Estonian society and encounter it with sensitivity and poise. We trace the country's turbulent history and try to see how the past has shaped the collective and personal values of today's Estonians. We look at the Estonian people at work, at play, and at home, and offer tips to help you get along with Estonian colleagues and acquaintances—without any awkward silences!

Key Facts

Official Name	*Eesti Vabariik* (Republic of Estonia)	
Capital City	Tallinn	Pop. 400,000
Main Cities and Towns	Tartu, Narva, Pärnu, Viljandi, Rakvere	
Area	28,102 sq. miles (45,226 sq km). This includes 1,500 islands in the Baltic Sea.	
Terrain	Flat, with large tracts of marshland and many lakes; heavily forested	
Climate	Temperate	
Currency	Kroon (EEK). The kroon is pegged to the euro at a rate of 15.65 EEK to 1 euro.	
Population	1.3 million. Population density approx. 30 people/sq km (2007)	
Ethnic Makeup	67.9% Estonian, 25.6% Russian, 6.5% other. "Other" includes Ukrainians, Belarussians, and Finns.	
National Languages	67.3% Estonian, 29.7% Russian, 3% other. Estonian is the official langauge.	
Religion	13.6% Evangelical Lutheran, 12.8% Orthodox, 1.4% other Christian	Most Estonians do not belong to any religious organization.

Government	Parliamentary republic, with one legislative house, the Riigikogu	The country is divided into 15 counties.
Media	There are three domestic television channels: ETV, Kanal 2, and TV3. Finnish stations can be picked up. Cable channels available	Main newspapers: *Õhtuleht, Postimees, Eesti Express, Äripläev*. There are two daily Russian-language papers: *Molodjozh Estonii* and *Vesti Dnja*.
Media: English-language	Some British and American newspapers are available, notably the *Financial Times*.	The weekly *Baltic Times* rounds up the week's news in Estonia, Latvia, and Lithuania.
Electricity	220 volts, 50 Hz. Standard European two-prong plugs are used.	British appliances need an adaptor; American appliances need an adaptor and a transformer.
Video/TV	Videos use the PAL system.	
Telephone	The country code for Estonia is 372. To dial out of Estonia, dial 00.	There are no area codes in Estonia. All numbers have seven digits.
Time Zone	Estonia is on Eastern European Time: 2 hours ahead of GMT, normally 7 hours ahead of US Eastern Standard Time, and 10 hours ahead of Pacific Standard Time.	In summer, Estonia is 3 hours ahead of GMT.

chapter one

LAND & PEOPLE

Bigger than Belgium but smaller than Slovakia, Estonia is the historical meeting point of East-West trading routes. Lying on the northwestern part of the rising East European platform, on the eastern shore of the Baltic Sea, south of the Gulf of Finland, Estonia shares borders with Latvia and Russia, with which it is still disputing territory illegally taken by Stalin at the end of the Second World War. The capital, Tallinn, is home to a fast-developing transit port. The country's low, flat, marshy terrain is sprinkled with more than a thousand natural and artificial lakes, one of which, near Tallinn, has given its name to the airport: Ülemiste.

Covering an area of about 17,462 square miles (45,226 square kilometers), Estonia has a population of around 1.3 million, making it one of Europe's most sparsely populated countries, with wide stretches of unspoiled natural landscape. This divides into two areas: the flat north, with a boulder-scattered coastline, and the mildly hilly south, around the skiing capital of Otepää. The highest point, at 1,043 feet (318 meters), is the modestly named Suur Munamägi (Great Egg Mountain), which is also the highest point in the Baltic region.

Estonia has 2,357 miles (3,794 kilometers) of coastline, characterized by bays, straits, and inlets, steep limestone cliffs along the Gulf of Finland, and a string of sandy white beaches to the west. There are 1,520 islands and islets, most of them small and uninhabited. The largest is Saaremaa ("island land"), followed by Hiiumaa, Muhu, and Vormsi. The Pärnu and Emajõgi ("Mother") are the most important of the country's rivers. The latter flows through Estonia's second city, the university town of Tartu. Most of the border with Russia slices through Lake Peipsi, which, at 1,373 square miles (3,555 square kilometers), is the largest lake in the land, and the fourth biggest in Europe. The second-largest lake is the fish-filled Võrtsjärv, which lies west of Tartu.

Marshland is prevalent in central and eastern Estonia; the best place for trekking through bogs is the peat-rich national park of Soomaa ("bog land"). About half the country is coated in

forest—mainly spruce, birch, and pine—and inhabited by elk, roe deer, beavers, boars, bears, lynxes, and wolves. Estonia has also become popular with bird-watchers, with Matsalu, on the western coast, perhaps the favorite venue for this activity. In the southeastern region of Tartumaa you can still find primeval forest that no longer exists in other parts of Europe. A popular area for following nature trails is Lahemaa ("land of bays"), a sprawling national park along the northern coast. Wooded meadows are particularly rich in flora: the meadow of Vahenurme, in the southwestern region of Pärnumaa, contains around seventy species of flora per square yard. Natural resources include peat, phosphorite, and oil shale, which provides more than 75 percent of the country's energy supply and is produced in northeast Estonia, near the border with Russia.

CLIMATE

Estonia's climate is temperate and humid, modified by air brought in by cyclonic winds from the North Atlantic. These bring cool air in summer and warm air in winter. The climate is more continental in the east and southeast, and generally milder in the western and northern coastal areas. The average temperature ranges from 61°F (16°C) on the islands to 63°F (17°C) inland in July (although temperatures in recent years have frequently reached the low thirties), and from 26°F (-3.5°C) on the islands to 18°F (-7.6°C) inland in February. The lowest temperature, -45°F (-43°C), was recorded in central Estonia in 1940.

The best time to visit Estonia is between May and September. The worst is November, when daylight is minimal and there is no guarantee of snow to brighten the gloom. The seasons are pronounced, and characterized most dramatically by changes in the amount of daylight. In midwinter, it gets dark around 3:00 p.m.; in June, it doesn't get dark at all, with eerie grey midnights and bright dawns. The wettest time is late summer. For those who like snow and winter sports, such as cross-country skiing through forests, the ideal month to visit is February. The sight of the frozen sea on a sunny winter morning, or splashed with pinks and purples at sunset, is unforgettable. Unfortunately, there is no longer any guarantee that it will freeze in winter. Forget vanity and wrap up well, with hat, gloves, and sturdy boots, or you will probably be scolded by warmly clad locals.

A BRIEF HISTORY

Owing in part to its strategic position, Estonia has had an eventful and tragic history, and has suffered dramatic population losses over the centuries due to famine, plague, war, deportation, and flight. The country has had a long history of successive invasions, occupations, and fragmentation. The outline that follows helps to convey what makes today's Estonia "Estonian," and what distinguishes it from nearby Russia and Finland.

Prehistory

Hunting and fishing communities similar to those in Latvia and southern Finland were present in this land from about 6,500 BCE. The Finno-Ugric ancestors of the Estonian people are thought to have settled in Baltic coastal territory five thousand years ago, after migrating from an area west of the Ural Mountains. There is controversy over their exact origins, but archaeologists believe that the most likely original "homeland" of these tribes was somewhere between the Volga River and Scandinavia. Whatever the facts, Estonians take great pride in telling you that they are thought to be one of the longest-settled peoples in Europe.

Agriculture and cattle- and sheep rearing appear to have been well established by 1,500 BCE. Some five hundred years on, a Finno-Ugric culture involving the creation of hill forts developed on agricultural lands and along trade routes such as the Emajõgi River. By contrast, the southern Baltic territory (most of present-day Latvia and Lithuania) was inhabited by Indo-European Balts.

The name "Aestii" ("Eesti" in Estonian) may come from "Aesti," a word used by Germanic people to describe those living northeast of the Vistula River. The first written reference to the "Aestii" people was made by Tacitus in 98 CE.

Knights of the Sword

The somewhat skeptical Estonians are proud to point out that their territory was one of the last patches of pagan Europe to be converted to

Christianity. There was fierce resistance to crusaders from northern Germany, who established a stronghold in Riga following Pope Celestine III's call for a crusade against the heathens of northern Europe in 1193. Estonia was finally defeated by the German Order of the Brothers of the Sword in 1217, after which the territory was split between the Livonian branch of the Teutonic Order, the Bishopric of Dorpat (now Tartu), and the Bishopric of Ösel-Wiek. The last corner of Estonia to be conquered was the island of Saaremaa—and the islanders are, of course, still proud of that. In 1219, Danish crusaders under the command of King Waldemar II landed in Estonia and defeated locals at the Battle of Lyndanisse. Despite the presence of a German-speaking ruling class, Tallinn was theoretically a Danish possession until 1293. During that time, Tallinn won its town charter, based on the Lübeck Law, in 1248, and in 1285 became a member of the Hanseatic League— the powerful confederation of free towns and cities that dominated the Baltic trade and its relations with Flanders and England—thus becoming one of the most prosperous towns in northern Europe.

In 1344, the Baltic German landowners quashed a popular rebellion on the island of Saaremaa and northern Estonia, today remembered as the St. George's Night Uprising. (A memorial to this stands on the highway to Narva, near Tallinn.) In 1345 the Danes sold Tallinn and their other lands in

northern Estonia to the
Teutonic Order. Russia
attempted but failed to
invade the territory in 1481
and 1558, the latter time
under Ivan the Terrible.
The well-established Baltic
German administrative
and commercial presence
in Estonia ensured the country's commitment to
the Protestant Reformation and continued, despite
various occupations, until the country achieved
self-determination following the First World War.

The "Good Old Swedish" Period
In 1561, as a consequence of the Livonian War,
Estonia became a Swedish dominion. When Ivan
the Terrible invaded the country, he was confronted
by an alliance of Poland-Lithuania and Sweden.
Sweden first gained control of northern Estonia.
Southern Estonia fell under Polish rule. By 1625, the
whole of the mainland had been conquered by the
Swedes. Although many locals starved to death
during periods of famine, when locally produced
food was transported to Sweden, most Estonians
fondly remember the rule of Gustavus Adolphus,
who in 1631 granted the downtrodden local
peasants and serfs greater autonomy from the
German nobility. Gustavus also opened the
prestigious university of Dorpat (now Tartu), which
attracted students from across Europe—though
not, initially, local Estonians.

The Turn of the Tsars

It was, once again, not the will of the Estonian people that decided what happened to their land next, but yet another international conflict: the Great Northern War (1700–21). On one side was Sweden, with help from the Ottomans; on the other, a coalition uniting Russia, Denmark-Norway, Saxony-Poland, and, from 1715, Prussia and Hanover. By the end of the war, Estonia had become a province of Russia—though still with a Baltic German ruling class—which had supplanted Sweden as the dominant power on the Baltic Sea.

It had long been Peter the Great's ambition to secure a "window on the west." As a result, the Finno-Ugric people of Estonia found themselves caught between the two very different cultures of Germany and Russia. Baltic German administrators continued to run the legal system, local government, the Lutheran Church, and education, but Russia owned the territory. Things here were rather different from the rest of the Russian empire. The "backwater" Baltic provinces were the first in the empire to see, in 1819, the abolition of serfdom, which allowed Estonian peasants to own their own land and to enjoy freedom of movement. This was celebrated fifty years later by the first Estonian song festival, held in Tartu.

National Awakening

Greater freedoms inevitably encouraged the trend for nationalism and self-determination that was spreading throughout Europe in the mid-nineteenth century. In Estonia, this was chiefly a cultural movement, encouraging the use of Estonian, not German, in schools, the creation of Estonian literature, poetry, and newspapers, and the song festivals that continue to this day. One of the leaders of this movement was the poet Lydia Koidula, whose father, J. W. Jannsen, had launched a daily Estonian-language newspaper in Pärnu in

1857. One of its main themes was the value of education, still treasured by Estonians today. Koidula's poetry remembers the past and hopes for a brighter future. Meanwhile F. R. Keutzwald, who was of Baltic-German origin, began compiling *Kalevipoeg*, a tale of heroism and "rising again" that was to become the Estonian national epic. It was published in both German and Estonian in 1861. Tsar Alexander III (1881–94), who did not much care for all this patriotic activity, introduced a government-sponsored policy of Russification. Many institutes, including the University of Tartu, had to conduct all their activities in Russian.

Inevitably, the revolution of 1905 had a huge impact on neighboring Estonia. Calls for freedom of the press and of assembly, and for universal franchise, went hand in hand with the demand for national autonomy. That year, scores of Estonian demonstrators were massacred by Tsarist troops just outside Tallinn's Old Town. During this unstable period (1905–17), Estonians dared to imagine that their country could become an independent state. Amid the chaos that followed the disintegration of the Russian empire, Russia's provisional government granted Estonia autonomy, but the path to independence was complicated by both Russian and German claims on the territory. The Bolsheviks outlawed Estonia's first popularly elected assembly, although this did not prevent it from proclaiming the Republic of Estonia on February 24, 1918—a date still celebrated as Independence Day. The following day, German troops invaded. They withdrew in November, enabling the formation of a provisional Estonian government. Within days, Soviet Russia invaded, beginning the Estonian War of Independence (1918–20), with stretched Estonian troops receiving support from the British navy and volunteers from Denmark, Finland, and Sweden. On New Year's Eve, 1919, Bolshevik Russia and the Republic of Estonia finally agreed to a truce, resulting in the Tartu Peace Treaty of February 2, 1920, according to which Russia renounced all claims to Estonia forever. The Republic of Estonia won international recognition and joined the League of Nations in 1921.

Independent Estonia

Democratic Estonia introduced a liberal constitution that proclaimed the supremacy of parliament, the Riigikogu. Land reforms ensured that the property of the Baltic nobility was redistributed to Estonians, many of them workers and peasants. Tartu University was now an Estonian university, with mainly Estonian students. Cultural and academic life thrived, and Estonia became the first country in Western Europe to guarantee cultural autonomy to minority groups, including Jews. The country found export markets, especially for agricultural products, in Western Europe and the USA, as well as the Soviet Union. The standard of living was soon higher than that in Finland.

The country's liberal political system was, however, shaken by the world economic crisis of 1929, which fueled both socialist and fascist extremism. Changes to the constitution in 1933 restricted the power of parliament and considerably strengthened the authority of the head of state, President Konstantin Päts. Estonia's policy of neutrality was sabotaged by the Nazi-Soviet Molotov-Ribbentrop Pact of 1939, according to which Germany and the Soviet Union agreed to assign Finland, Estonia, Latvia, Lithuania, and Poland to either Soviet or Nazi spheres of influence. The Soviet Union offered Estonia an ultimatum: accept Soviet military bases on Estonian territory, or be invaded. Päts complied, and by the end of June the following year, the Soviet occupation was secure. The Soviet Union demanded the formation of a pro-Soviet puppet government, followed by "elections," for which only pro-Communist candidates were allowed to run. The new "parliament" proclaimed the Estonian Socialist Republic in 1940 and asked to become part of the USSR. The occupation and annexation of Estonia was considered illegal by the United States and other Western states, including Britain.

Soviet and Nazi Occupations

Soviet Estonia's immediate priority was to eliminate all "enemies of the people." More than eight thousand people, including politicians and members of the military, were arrested and executed in Estonia or transported to prison and labor camps in Russia. President Päts died in a psychiatric institution in Kalinin in 1956. During the mass deportations of June 1941, about ten thousand civilians, including five hundred members of the 4,500-strong Jewish community, were sent to Russia, many to Siberia. Women and children were separated from the men, many of whom perished in labor camps, their fate often unknown to surviving relatives until the 1960s. Half of the civilians deported did not survive the harsh conditions imposed on them in Russia. After the German invasion of Russia on June 22, more than thirty thousand Estonian men were transported to Russia, supposedly to join the Soviet army. Nearly half died in "labor battalions."

When the German army reached Estonia in July, many Estonians had become so appalled by the Soviet terror that they greeted Nazi soldiers with flowers, naively believing that Germany would restore their country's independence. In fact, its aim was straightforward: occupation. One of the Nazi priorities was to make Estonia "Jew-free." Around half of the Jewish population escaped to the Soviet Union. Those who stayed were rounded up and executed by the *Einsatzkommandos* with the aid of local collaborators; only a handful are thought to have survived the Soviet and Nazi occupations. Germany also opened concentration and labor camps for Jews from other countries in Estonia. As Allied victory over Germany became likely, the Nazi regime called on Estonians to join the fight against the Soviets; many did, in the hope, naive once again, that Estonian independence could be restored. A volunteer legion became the 20th Waffen Grenadier Division of the SS (1st Estonian). As the Germans retreated, the last prime minister of independent Estonia formed a government and asked for recognition from the Allies; but the Soviet Union reinvaded. Air raids wrecked the border city of Narva and more than 30 percent of Tallinn's residential area. Ruins from this period can still be seen in Tallinn, on Harju Street, but many developers want to use this land. By the autumn of 1944, Soviet authority was secured and mass arrests and executions of "enemies of the people" recommenced.

Estonia lost around one in five of its population as a result of the Second World War, including eighty thousand people who fled to the West, many to Sweden, where an Estonian government in exile continued to exist until 1992. To some extent, the

Second World War is still being played out in
Estonia, with some Estonians objecting to the
continued presence of Soviet war memorials, in
particular the statue of the "Soldier Liberator" that
until recently stood outside the National Library in
Tallinn, while Estonian veterans from the German
army call for a monument that honors them. To
date, the Estonian authorities have quashed
attempts to create the latter, but in 2007 the
government moved the statue of the "Soldier
Liberator" to a military cemetery outside Tallinn
(see page 53).

Since Estonians were forcibly recruited into both
the Soviet and Nazi armies (the most tragic being
the battles on both sides of the Narva River, in
which Estonians were forced to fight each other), it
is wrong to assume that anyone who fought for
either side was necessarily doing so for ideological
reasons. The predicament of being Estonian during
the Soviet and Nazi occupations is captured with
insight and humanity by the Estonian writer Jaan
Kross, himself imprisoned during both (see *The
Conspiracy and Other Stories*). Since 2002, Estonia
has commemorated Holocaust Remembrance Day
on January 27. In August 2006, a law against
inciting ethnic hatred was proposed in Estonia. This
would have banned the use of Soviet, Communist,
and Nazi symbols, with the penalties for breaching
it a heavy fine of up to EEK18,000 ($1,500), or
arrest. It was vetoed by the President on the ground
that it would be unconstitutional, and was seen by
some commentators as electioneering.

Soviet Estonia, 1944–91

The Communist Party of the Estonian Soviet Socialist Republic now controlled the republic. Resistance to the occupation continued, most dramatically in the shape of the Forest Brothers ("Metsavennad") guerrilla movement. This consisted of partisan groups, mainly in rural areas, that engaged Soviet forces in battle. Some members had fled to the woods several years previously to escape being drafted into either the Nazi or the Soviet army. The last forest brother killed himself when discovered by the KGB in 1978. In an attempt to quash other forms of resistance, the Soviet regime deported more than twenty thousand people to Russia in March 1949.

The "thaw" that followed Stalin's death in 1953 made it easier for Estonians to make contact with foreign countries. A ferry connection opened between Tallinn and Helsinki. Those living in northern Estonia could illicitly access Finnish television, which provided a valuable window to the Western world. None the less, the Brezhnev era in particular engendered feelings of stagnation and despair, well captured by the stark, haunting music of the Estonian composer Arvo Pärt in the 1970s. It is hard for foreigners to understand that there were genuine fears for cultural survival among Estonians, but this was the era of increased Russification, with thousands of Russian-speaking migrant workers from across the Soviet Union sent to Estonia, many working in industries established to meet the needs of the Soviet Union rather than those of the local population. This led to resentment and fear. One visible legacy of this part-economic, part-political policy was the increase in the building of soulless, Soviet-style high-rise apartment buildings: Lasnamäe, in Tallinn, is an egregious example.

Thankfully, change was not so long in coming. Tallinn's relatively liberal climate, together with the emergence of the Polish Solidarity movement in the 1980s, encouraged Estonians to support a more radical program of *perestroika* (restructuring) than the Russian President, Gorbachev, had intended. As in the other Baltic States, a popular movement (in Estonia, the Popular Front) emerged in the late 1980s. An anti-Soviet Green movement, fueled by damage caused to the environment, for example by the Soviet army, was also formed, while more outspoken dissidents established the Estonian National Independence Party. Estonia's Supreme Soviet began to acquire regional autonomy by adopting laws to introduce economic independence and to reinstate Estonian as the official language. Most Russian-speakers were initially unconvinced about the benefits of independence. Moscow-backed attempts to instill fear, via rallies orchestrated by members of the local Communist military-industrial complex, failed, however, to gain significant support.

In the end, it was the grassroots Estonian Citizens' Committees Movement (1989) that called for the registration of all prewar citizens of the Republic of Estonia, and their descendants, to join a Congress of Estonia. Its main argument was that the Soviet occupation was illegal and that the Republic of Estonia had never ceased to exist de jure, only de facto. The run-up to the restoration of independence was confusing, with parallel elections held by the 900,000-strong Congress and the Estonian Supreme Soviet. Pressured by the Estonian Committee elected by the Congress, the coalition of left and centrist parties that now dominated the Supreme Soviet restored the name of the "Republic of Estonia," and declared that the only laws valid in Estonia would be those adopted by the Supreme Soviet. Western journalists were impressed by the dignity and restraint shown during this politically complex time, when determination to avoid confrontation was paramount. There were no bloody crackdowns, as in Latvia and Lithuania in 1991. The final catalyst was the hard-line coup in August in Moscow, and the consequent disintegration of the Soviet Union. Estonia

redeclared its independence on August 20, 1991. The first Western state to recognize it was Iceland (hence "Iceland Square" near the present-day Foreign Ministry building), quickly followed by others, including the USA. The Soviet occupation was only fully over, however, when the last Russian troops withdrew in 1994. A decade later, Estonia joined NATO and the European Union. It now has five MEPs.

The Singing Revolution

The four-year-long peaceful transition to the restoration of independence in Estonia was named after the first mass, openly anti-occupation Song Festival in the summer of 1988, when as many as 300,000 people gathered at the Song Bowl grounds between Kadriorg and Pirita to boldly and calmly sing songs banned during the Soviet occupation. This followed the signing in April of a declaration by Estonian intellectuals calling for genuine *perestroika*.

Estonia Today

Today, Estonia is resolutely Westward-looking, although investment continues to pour in from Russia—some of it via money laundering. International institutions have described the country as one of the most attractive states to invest in, thanks to the famous flat-tax system and liberal business laws, in particular the waiving of corporation tax for companies that reinvest profits in Estonia. The relative prosperity brought by several straight years of double-digit growth has seen property values soar, especially in Tallinn's Old Town. Not everyone, however, is doing well. The pressure to earn, or simply to survive, especially for retirees, is intense. Wealth is slowly beginning to filter down, and more and more Russian-speakers are benefiting from the new Estonia, especially in the service sector, and opting for Estonian passports. The country has made huge strides in building up a civil society, but there is some way to go in establishing a truly open-minded and tolerant society where difference and disability are fully respected.

The election as President, in 2006, of a Westward-looking Estonian exile, Toomas Hendrik Ilves (born in Sweden, raised in Canada), who gave up his US passport to join Estonian politics in the 1990s, confirmed Estonia's commitment to Europe. This irks Russia, which has always found it hard to accept that Estonia should be outside its sphere of influence. Relations with Russia are uneasy, with drawn-out border checks common, journalists denied access to international events in Russia, and the agreed upon border still not legally adopted by Russia. Most Estonians are deeply suspicious of Big Brother next door, and are unimpressed, although not surprised, by President Vladimir Putin's increasing authoritarianism and the way he seems to tolerate hard-line, xenophobic Russian nationalist movements while condemning Estonian "nationalism." Now that Estonia has an official voice within the EU, however, Russia is finding it increasingly difficult to draw mileage out of the argument that Estonians don't respect the rights of Russians in Estonia.

ESTONIA'S CITIES

Although Estonia is largely a rural, forested country, the majority of its population (nearly 70 percent) lives in towns, principally in Tallinn and its rapidly expanding suburbs. Villages and small towns are often disconcertingly strung out along two sides of the "main" road, with no obvious center or square. Given the large areas of uninhabited terrain, and the Estonian fondness for space and privacy, farms and homes tend to be placed well away from each other, bounded by neat hedges, and with extensive gardens dotted with apple and lilac trees. You can still see remnants of the Soviet era in the shape of gray, abandoned collective farm buildings or residential blocks, many of which have been spruced up and made more secure. There has been a building boom in recent years, resulting in new housing, office blocks, and shopping complexes. The main industrial areas are in and around Tallinn, and in the northeast.

Tallinn

Tallinn (pronounced, like most Estonian words, with a strong emphasis on the first syllable and a light "t" sound) is Estonia's capital and, even under occupation, was known as a "Western," liberal outpost of the Soviet empire. Its name allegedly derives from "Taani-linn"

(Danish town, or castle), although some believe it comes from "tali-linn" (winter town) or "talu-linna"

(farmstead town). Its German name, Reval, used by the Swedes and adopted in Russian, was replaced by Tallinn when Estonia declared its independence (1918). It derives from the name of the surrounding Estonian county, once known as Rävala. Today, Tallinn is the commercial and cultural center of Estonia. Its population is about 400,000, of whom 55 percent are Estonian and 37 percent "Russian," or "Russian-speaking."

Tallinn's beautifully austere limestone Town Hall is the last surviving Gothic town hall in northern Europe, and an eloquent symbol of the city's wealth at the time of the Hanseatic League. Much of what you see today dates to the early fifteenth century, except the Renaissance spire. Tallinn consists of Toompea (Cathedral Hill), which was historically the seat of bishops, the Teutonic Order, and the nobility—and is now home to the Estonian government and parliament—and the prettily preserved Vanna Linn (Old Town), where medieval trade flourished and a strong city government emerged. Kesklinn (Center Town), which grew up in the nineteenth and twentieth centuries, is sprinkled with examples of 1930s and Soviet architecture, as well as shiny new office and residential blocks. One of the hallmarks of the Old Town, a UNESCO World Heritage Site, is the almost intact string of fortifications dotted with russet turrets, which encloses a colorful complex of cobbled streets and old merchant houses.

Tallinn is set to be European Capital of Culture in 2011, along with Turku, in Finland.

Tartu

Tartu, in southeast Estonia, the country's second city, has a population of a little more than 100,000. First recorded in writing in 1030, Tartu has long been a more-or-less friendly rival to Tallinn. City of *vaim* (spirit), it likes to define itself in opposition to Tallinn, city of *võim* (power); Tallinn may be the *pealinn* (capital, literally "head town"), but Tartu is *peagalinn* (the city "with a head"). Most recently, Tartu, which joined the Hanseatic League before Tallinn, competed for the right to be European Capital of Culture in 2011.

Famous for its university, established by Gustavus Adolphus of Sweden in 1632, Tartu, also known as Dorpat (from the old fort of Tarbatu) is renowned for innovation, particularly in linguistics and science. Many of the  country's movers and shakers are graduates, and there is an influential "old boys' network."

The heart of the city, including the main university buildings and the offices of the Estonian Ministry for Education, is situated west of the Emajõgi River and spreads uphill to Toomemägi (Toome Hill), site of the dramatic red-brick ruins of St. Peter and St. Paul Cathedral, which was completed in the fifteenth century and destroyed during the Livonian War in the sixteenth. The Town Hall square, ravaged by fires in the eighteenth century, is now mainly neoclassical in appearance.

One of the city's most treasured possessions is the Gothic, red-brick Jaani Kirik (St. John's Church), famous for its delicate terra-cotta figures. The city, closed to foreigners during the Soviet occupation because of the presence of a Soviet air base, was spruced up to host the international Hansa days in 2005. There are plans to rebuild the beloved eighteenth-century stone bridge across the Emajõgi, which was bombed by the Russians during the Second World War. Tartu has a large and lively foreign community, thanks to the university.

Pärnu

Known as Estonia's "summer capital" because of its fine white-sand, pine-backed beach and vibrant summer cultural program, Pärnu is situated in southwestern Estonia, toward Riga. It has a modest population of just over 44,000, but has long been a popular health resort, its mud baths and therapies attracting Finns and Russians in search of cures for anything from disorders of the joints to problems with the central nervous system. Pärnu is also famed for its thriving theater scene, the Museum of New Art, and the prestigious David Oistrakh music festival, frequented by the conductor Neeme Järvi, who also supported the creation of an impressive new concert hall, completed in 2002. One of the city's most famous citizens was Carl Robert Jakobson, an educator, journalist, and leading figure in the national awakening movement; another was the poet Lydia Koidula. The low-lying town, with a spattering of seventeenth- and eighteenth-century

architecture, straddles the southern side of the
Pärnu River. One of its most distinctive buildings is
the lemon-and-green Orthodox church of
Catherine the Great.

Narva

In the northeastern corner of Estonia, on the banks
of the Narva River, this was once a beautiful
baroque city, but much of it was destroyed during
the Second World War. Its most dramatic sight
today is the thirteenth-
century castle, which
acquired its present
appearance in the early
fifteenth century. It faces
Ivangorod Fortress, built
in the late fifteenth

century, which stands in equally challenging fashion
across the river on the Russian side of the border
(though it was part of Narva before the Second
World War). When Estonia lost its independence,
Narva's population changed as sharply as its
appearance. Estonians who had fled the damage
were not allowed to return. Once predominantly
Estonian, its population of 67,000 is now almost
entirely Russian-speaking, with most being ethnic
Russians, including Soviet-era immigrants from the
former U.S.S.R. and their descendants. About
28,000 have Estonian passports, with a similar
number bearing Russian passports. One of the
challenges for Estonia is that as many as 17,000
residents have no determined citizenship. The

largest industries are textiles, power engineering, and the manufacture of clothing, furniture, and building materials.

Viljandi

Traditionally an agricultural town, Viljandi, in southern Estonia, is historically home to famously boastful, well-to-do farmers, the so-called "Mulgi." With a population of 22,000, it differs significantly from other Estonian towns because of its hills. Like any Estonian town worth its salt, it has medieval castle ruins. Its most famous sight, however, is the suspension bridge nestling in the hills, given to the town by a Baltic-German baron in 1928. His family used it as a route to the chapel in the castle. The town hosts an internationally respected folk festival in July. Its industries include the production of textiles, timber, and construction materials, food processing, electronics, and printing. Viljandi Lake is a popular recreation spot. Curiously, the county of Viljandi is the only one in the country where there are more pigs than people.

Rakvere

Like all Estonian towns and cities, the modest but plucky northern town of Rakvere, which made a brave but doomed bid for European Cultural Capital 2011, has had a turbulent past and suffered various invasions and occupations. One of the chief attractions of this town of 17,000 souls is the romantically ruined castle, built in the fifteenth century. Modern Rakvere, whose intriguing motto is "Full of power," is quietly thriving and has attracted investors from Finland, Denmark, and Britain, mainly in the fields of food and wood processing.

Haapsalu

Though small in terms of population (11,000), the western coastal town of Haapsalu, midway between Tallinn and Pärnu, is steeped in faded Tsarist-era charm. Pretty nineteenth- and early-twentieth-century houses, some of them rather dilapidated, are decorated with lacy wooden carvings. The chief attraction is the wooden Kuursaal (entertainment hall) on the waterfront. It is historically significant as the place where a military doctor, Carl Abraham Hunnius, founded the first well-researched mud-cure resort in 1825. News of this soon spread to Russia, and Haapsalu began to attract aristocrats from St. Petersburg. The town was so popular with the Tsars that an especially long train station was built to accommodate arriving royals; the station is no longer in use, but the town remains a spa center. Tchaikovsky's bench, on the promenade, recalls the composer's summer sojourn here. You can sit on it and press buttons to hear excerpts of his music.

Otepää

Tiny Otepää (which may mean "bear's head," in memory of an early fortress that was supposedly shaped like the head of a bear) is set in the southern hills of Estonia's "little Switzerland." It has just 2,000 inhabitants, but attracts many visitors in winter, when it becomes the country's principal skiing and winter-sports destination. It is therefore known as the country's "winter capital." Holiday cottages may also be rented in warmer months, when Lake Pühajärv ("Holy Lake") is a popular summer spot, thanks to its small, sandy beaches, pine-shaded paths, and picnic areas. The lake was blessed by the Dalai Lama in 1991.

GOVERNMENT AND POLITICS

Estonia is a parliamentary republic based on a constitution adopted in 1992. The national-level, one-chamber Parliament (Riigikogu) comprises 101 directly elected members, who serve for four-year terms. The head of state is the president, who is elected by the Parliament for a five-year term and can run for office only twice. If, as happened in the 2006 presidential elections, no presidential candidate wins two-thirds of the vote after three rounds of voting in Parliament, an electoral assembly consisting of Parliament and members of local government elects the president from the two highest-scoring candidates. The prime minister, who has much greater powers, is nominated by the president and approved by Parliament. The government is formed by the prime minister, and then appointed by the president after approval by Parliament. At the last general election, in March 2007, the biggest party was Reform, with 27.8 percent of the vote and 31 seats, followed by the Center Party, with 26.1 percent and 29 seats, IRL,

with 17.9 percent and 19 seats, the Social
Democrats, with 10.6 percent and 10 seats, the
Greens, with 7.1 percent and 6 seats, and the
Estonian People's Union, again with 7.1 percent and
6 seats. The current prime minister is Andrus Ansip.
There are twenty women in the 101-seat
parliament, and three women in the thirteen-
member cabinet.

Voting is universal for all Estonian citizens aged
eighteen years and over, and is not compulsory. All
Estonian citizens aged twenty-one and over have
the right to run for election. Resident noncitizens
and those who have lived permanently in Estonia
for at least five years before an election may vote in
local elections, but cannot run for office. Citizens
vote in local and parliamentary elections, held every
four years, respectively in October and
March. The system for both is one of
proportional representation. The
electoral threshold of 5 percent means
that smaller parties do not get seats in
Parliament. In 2003, six of the eleven
parties that took part gained seats.

Voter turnout is low, at about 60 percent, and was at
its lowest since the restoration of Estonian
independence during the first European
Parliamentary elections (2004), in which just 27
percent of the electorate voted.

The Riigikohus (National Court) is the supreme
court, with nineteen justices. The President
nominates its chair, who is then appointed for life
by the Parliament. It is thought that approximately

100,000 Russian-speaking residents who are not citizens (that is, they have not chosen Estonian nationality) cannot vote in general elections.

Regional Government
Estonia has fifteen administrative divisions, or counties (*maakonnad*), as shown below.

County	Capital
Harjumaa	Tallinn
Hiiumaa	Kardla
Ida-Virumaa	Johvi
Järvamaa	Paide
Jõgevamaa	Jõgeva
Läänemaa	Haapsalu
Lääne-Virumaa	Rakvere
Pärnumaa	Pärnu
Põlvamaa	Põlva
Raplamaa	Rapla
Saaremaa	Kuressaare
Tartumaa	Tartu
Valgamaa	Valga
Viljandimaa	Viljandi
Võrumaa	Võru

For local elections, there are twelve multi-mandate districts with six to twelve mandates; these are distributed according to the number of citizens eligible to vote in each electoral district.
Candidates may be nominated by a registered political party or run independently. For the local

elections of October 2005, Estonia employed the largest e-voting scheme ever run by an EU country. To participate, voters needed an electronic card-reader and an identity card with its own unique number. They were then able to vote online anywhere in the world.

The Mayor of Tallinn, elected by a city council of sixty-three elected councilors for a four-year term, is responsible for general administration, law enforcement, city development plans, the city's budget, and relations with state and government organizations and with city district administrations; and represents the City of Tallinn at home and abroad.

Can the Word "Social" be Acceptable in Politics?
The current president is a member of the Social Democrat Party, which changed its name from "People's Party Möödukad" in 2005, in the hope that "social" was no longer a word distrusted for sounding like "socialist." With six seats, it is the smallest party in Parliament, but three of Estonia's five MEPs are Social Democrats. As this suggests, a growing number of citizens are reflecting that, following the radically liberal financial policies that characterized the early years of restored independence, it is time for a fairer distribution of wealth.

Although a grassroots "Green" movement was very strong in the late 1980s and early 1990s, the Greens lost ground to the big political parties that began to emerge in the early 1990s.

THE ECONOMY

After 1920, the first Republic of Estonia built up its economy with dramatic success. Following the reestablishment of independence in 1991, the country lost no time in rapidly transforming itself into a modern, Westward-looking market economy with a highly developed information technology sector (a "Silicon Valley on the Baltic Sea," according to the New York Times). The Soviet-era heavy industries have been replaced by service, light, textile, and food industries.

A Clean Slate

Despite the difficulties of disentangling its economy from Russia and establishing a Westward-looking market economy, Estonia introduced radical reforms to create a highly liberal economic climate that soon earned the country the title of "Baltic Tiger." Businesses are exempt from corporate tax if they reinvest in business in Estonia (although there is a growing belief that this will have to change within the next few years). There is a flat 24 percent tax rate for all, with no inheritance tax. The Estonian kroon was pegged to the German mark in 1992, then to the euro. Although the state budget is balanced and public debt is low (3 percent of GDP), the current-account deficit is high. Unemployment hovers at 9 percent, and is highest in northeastern Estonia (partly because not all Russian-speakers can speak the country's official language) and in rural areas (following the collapse of the collective farms). Tallinn attracts by far the greatest share of foreign investment. It is the richest region, and continues to reap the benefits of its harbor and trading ports, in particular the warm-water Muuga. Tourism and related services are the fastest-growing sectors.

At the national level, Estonia's economy is principally dependent on services, transportation, manufacturing, and trade. Natural resources include oil shale, limestone, peat, and phosphorite. Agriculture accounts for 4.5 percent of GDP and employs about 5 percent of the workforce, a drop of 9 percent since 1992.

According to Statistics Estonia, industrial production in industry and manufacturing grew by 11 percent between May 2005 and 2006, with manufacturing growth most pronounced in food, wood, and metal. Retail sales went up by 22 percent, and GDP rose by 11.7 percent year-on-year in the first quarter of 2006, mainly because of increasing domestic demand and growing private consumption and expenditure. Imports of goods and services increased faster than exports, respectively by more than 21 percent and 17 percent.

ESTONIA IN EUROPE

When Estonia held its referendum on joining the EU in 2003, many Estonians were suspicious: why leave one large (Soviet) union to join another? There was also fear that prices would soar as a result. Pro-EU lobbyists had some difficulty in persuading the electorate that these two unions are radically different, the first being unpredictable and autocratic, the second governed by the rule of law, democracy, and free speech. In the end, it was an interest in security that persuaded many voters to choose EU membership, with the EU seen as a buffer against Estonia's unpredictable neighbor. The yes vote, however, was 66.8 percent in Estonia, well below that in Lithuania (91.1 percent). Joining the union hugely boosted Estonia's international image and underlined its exit from the Russian sphere of influence, hence President Ilves's declaration, irksome to President Putin, that Estonia would deal with Russia via the European Union.

Estonia has six MEPs (three of whom are women), including three members of the Social Democrat Party (aligned with the European Socialists), one for the patriotic Pro Patria Union (aligned with the European Peoples' Party), one for the Center Party, and one for the Reform Party (both of the Alliance of Liberals and Democrats). Within the EU, Estonia tends to align itself with Scandinavia and Britain, rather than with Germany or France.

As one observer put it, "nobody talks much about the EU any more," although there are concerns that joining has led to rising property prices and a brain drain to other EU countries where salaries are higher, accompanied by a feeling of irritation that countries like France and Germany did not grant free movement to Estonian workers. A huge practical problem is the number of construction workers who have left the country, making it difficult to find builders.

EU citizens living and working in Estonia are, however, generally very welcome. Tallinn is a comfortable and manageable city in which to live, with a good transportation system. Locals, particularly in Tallinn, have a good knowledge of languages, including English and Finnish. It would, however, be sensitive not to use Russian unless you are certain that someone is a Russian-speaker, or comfortable with speaking Russian.

ESTONIA IN THE WORLD

Estonia is a member of NATO, the United Nations, the EU, the Western European Union, the Organization for Security and Co-operation in Europe, the World Trade Organization, the International Monetary Fund, World Bank, the European Bank for Reconstruction and Development, and the World Customs Organization, and is an observer member of the Organization of American States. It has taken part in a number of UN peacekeeping operations, including the Balkans, Afghanistan, and Iraq.

One issue of international concern is the country's border with Russia. In 2005, Russia refused to sign the border treaty that it agreed upon with Estonia in 1996. Estonia wants recognition of the fact that the Soviet Union had occupied the country in breach of the 1920 Treaty of Tartu, and therefore illegally annexed parts of Estonian territory, including parts of the Narva region. Estonia has, however, agreed to concede some of this illegally annexed territory. Russia demands better accommodation of Estonia's Russian-speaking population.

The predominantly state-controlled Moscow media jumps at any opportunity to portray Estonians as "fascists," and it is worth remembering that much of the coverage of the Baltic States stems from foreign journalists based in Moscow, whose stories may be influenced by the Russian media. That said, Estonians can make mistakes, and with veterans of the Second World War still alive, the issue of Nazi "collaboration" still cuts deep. In commemorating the suffering of Estonians forcibly recruited into Hitler's and Stalin's armies, some people forget that the swastika is an offensive symbol to the civilized world. An effort in 2005 to erect a monument to an Estonian soldier in Nazi uniform in a tiny village near Pärnu drew worldwide condemnation, much to the amazement of some of its promoters who, typically, dug in their heels. In the end, the authorities sensibly removed the monument. Many people still feel their country suffered more under Stalin than under Hitler. However, compared with the emergence of apparently unpoliced neo-Nazi nationalists in Russia, who orchestrate the killings of non-Slav residents, there is little or no organized racism in Estonia.

There is an increasing drug-abuse problem in Estonia, with opiates and cannabis being shipped from southwest Asia and the Caucasus through Russia, cocaine from Latin America to Western Europe and Scandinavia, and synthetic drugs from Western Europe to Scandinavia. There is also concern about money laundering relating to organized crime and the use of the gambling sector to launder money.

VALUES & ATTITUDES

Several factors determine the values that Estonians hold and the way they approach life. The first is a keen awareness of the fact that Estonians and their language have survived despite occupation and oppression, and despite being so few in number. To be "Estonian" usually means being able to speak Estonian, for this obscure, singsong language is treasured. National pride is strong, but goes hand-in-hand with a feeling of vulnerability.

SO SMALL, SO MISUNDERSTOOD . . .

Much about the Estonian temperament stems from being a "small" nation (in terms of population, if not territory), wedged between larger, often hostile powers. Estonians have a keen sense of history: to laugh about the country's painful past would be poor in taste; too many people have firsthand experience of tragedy and atrocity. Countries that have never feared annihilation may balk at the locals' unalloyed patriotism, or at the number of flags that fly on significant historical anniversaries, but such patriotism is not chauvinistic; it is a recognition of survival and, more recently, dramatic economic progress. Pride is always taken in what a "little" country can achieve, such as winning three gold medals in the 2006 Winter Olympics (three more than Finland, Estonians like to point out). Estonians often appear self-deprecating, but are quietly proud and confident underneath.

There is a strong feeling of being misunderstood, particularly in a world where Big Brother Russia delights in giving Estonia a bad press, usually by dwelling on the alleged "abuse" of the rights of Russian-speakers in the country. (Ask these so-called victims what they think about living in a country that is doing well, and you are likely to get a very different story.) The downside is that Estonians, once they get going, can rant at foreigners, dishing out phrases such as "you don't understand," or "you have never been occupied." You could be forgiven for thinking that they don't want you to understand. Closely linked to survival is the "quality" of stubbornness. Being "small" also explains why Estonians tend to integrate when living abroad. In this sense, they are outward-looking and not at all provincial.

Estonians are individualists, excelling at solo sports such as cross-country skiing, javelin, and wrestling. At Tallinn's open-air rural architecture museum, Rocca al Mare, you can see how widely spaced the farm buildings traditionally were, guaranteeing privacy and solitude. Estonians tend to be modest about individual achievements, in keeping with their outwardly low-key behavior. They are not ostentatious or flashy, although, increasingly, status comes with the size of one's home and recognizable brands of clothes. "Keeping up with the neighbors" has always provided strong motivation.

THE LEGACY OF OCCUPATION AND TRADE
Estonia owes its turbulent past to the strategic value of its port capital, Tallinn, which has always been a meeting point for different cultures. Various occupations have resulted in a blend of caution, anti-authoritarianism, adaptability, inner resilience, and pragmatism. You will rarely come across a fanatical Estonian.

The introspective Estonians are surprisingly spontaneous when it comes to organizing social events, often inviting you to an event or party at the last minute; or, if you are a friend from abroad, reluctant to fix a date to meet until you are physically in the country. The same behavior is expected of you. For some, this is a legacy of the Soviet days, when it was considered dangerous to discuss sensitive subjects over potentially bugged phones, and when dropping in unannounced on a friend was common. Many people over the age of forty still have an automatic "censor reflex" in their minds. Surprisingly "Soviet" too, perhaps, is the lack of public politeness: people rarely hold doors open for others, even for parents with strollers, although, if you ask for help, the response will usually be gracious. In addition, because Finnish TV could be picked up illicitly in northern Estonia, including Tallinn, many Estonians are fluent in Finnish, and generally know far more about Finns than their Finno-Ugric cousins know about them.

Memories are short. There is already "nostalgia" for the Soviet days. This is not just a form of amnesia, but a fondness for the days when friendship was vital, when time was less precious because you got paid whatever you did, and when money was less important, as there was hardly anything to buy. The pressure to get on and make up for lost time is intense. Many believe such nostalgia is insensitive, if understandable. Recent polls show most Estonians dream, above all, of having more money. Women, in particular, can be strikingly tough and materialistic.

LANGUAGE AND IDENTITY

Estonians have often described themselves by highlighting how different they are from the occupier: they are not Russian, German, or even Scandinavian. As one of the Baltic States, they are keen to show that they are different from Latvians and Lithuanians. Superficially, one can describe Estonians as the northernmost Balts, with a reputation for being cool, hardheaded, and less whimsical than their southern neighbors. Ironically, there is no such thing as a "pure" Estonian, given past population loss through

famine, plagues, and war, and the flow of
incoming settlers from Scandinavia, Russia,
Poland, and even mercenaries from Scotland.
Even the most patriotic Estonian will admit that
the waves of immigration and foreign influence
have created a mixed people. Hence the
importance of language as a measure of identity.

"Not Russian" is the strongest legacy from the
Soviet era, when thousands of Russian-speaking
workers from across the Soviet Union were sent to
work in Estonia, for economic and political
reasons. In the late 1980s and early 1990s, there
was suspicion that "Russian-speakers" (a broad
term including Ukrainians, Belarusians, Russian-
speaking Georgians, and so on) would not
support the restoration of Estonian
independence. After the restoration, the large
population of Russian-speaking residents with
Soviet passports had to choose between Russian
and Estonian passports. Sixteen years later, many
Russian-speakers who settled during the Soviet
era still complain that they have to take an
Estonian-language test to acquire an Estonian
passport. If they have friends and relatives in
Russia, however, it makes traveling there more
complicated, because of the hassle of obtaining
expensive visas. Some Estonians concede that
Estonian-language teaching should be more
accessible and affordable, but most believe that if
Russian-speakers want to live in Estonia, they
should learn Estonian, which is the only official
language. The government has made efforts to

speed up and simplify access to citizenship, although the language test remains mandatory. Since 1998, all children born in Estonia after February 25, 1992, and whose parents have lived in the country for at least five years, are granted automatic citizenship.

Ethnic tension arose in 1996 over the Soviet statue of the "Soldier-Liberator," which used to stand outside the National Library in Tallinn. Estonians saw this as a symbol of occupation because there was no battle in Tallinn: Soviet forces reinvaded following the departure of German troops. An Estonian flag was raised on this monument, which was subsequently placed under police protection. Russian-speakers were not amused when the policemen set up "foosball" there to pass the time.

Tension flared again in 2007, following the statue's removal to a military cemetery, after the Estonian government claimed that it had become a focus for national extremism by both Russians and Estonians. There was extensive rioting, looting, and vandalism by Russian youths. Many Estonians believe that the Kremlin, from where thousands of cyber attacks were launched on Estonian government Web sites within hours of the rioting, had a hand in this. Rioters also besieged the Estonian embassy in Moscow, which the Kremlin was apparently unable to protect.

Most Estonians over the age of thirty have little contact with "Russian-speakers." This led to bemusement during the 2006 presidential elections: many Estonians said that everyone they knew favored the Western-thinking candidate Toomas Hendrik Ilves. They could not understand the popularity of the ambitious former Communist Party politician Edgar Savisaar, who has traditionally attracted the "Russian vote." Foreigners may be perplexed by this mutual lack of interest in how the "others" live. Those who befriend Russian-speakers, especially those who speak no Estonian, may be viewed with suspicion or incomprehension by Estonians. There is more social interaction in artistic and intellectual circles, and among the young. Increasingly, Estonians refer to "our Russians," and Russian-speakers to "our Estonia."

There is a widely recognized need to offer better Estonian-language teaching to Russian schoolchildren, while respecting the richness of Russian culture, which has a long pre-Soviet history in Estonia. Tallinn Pedagogical University and Tartu University both have Russian-language departments. There are several Russian-language newspapers and magazines, a Russian-language portal (Delfi), regular Russian cultural and news programs on Estonian television, and four Russian-language radio stations. Tallinn's Russian Drama Theater has an excellent reputation, and attracts Estonian theatergoers. The predominantly Russian-speaking town of Narva has its own symphony orchestra. In Tallinn, in particular, there is an audience for Russian rock bands.

ANTIAUTHORITARIANISM

Estonians tend to be skeptical of authority. They are independent-minded, dislike being told what to do, and generally mistrust politicians, often referring to their actions as "childish." Tax evasion is common, and many Estonians juggle more than one job to keep up with growing expenses. Citizens do, however, tend to be law-abiding and disciplined, despite some erratic driving. In business, Estonia is one of the most transparent and least corrupt former Communist countries.

MOVING ON, MOVING UP

Education is highly valued, partly because, for so many years, Estonians were "peasants," unlike their educated occupiers. Education has always been seen as a way of getting ahead. On September 1, "back to school" day, flags fly, and immaculately dressed children offer flowers to their class teachers. There is a deep respect for books. The official literacy rate is 100 percent. While other nations may be obsessed with home improvement, Estonians tend to focus on self-improvement: you never know what upsets lie around the corner, despite the reassuring presence of NATO planes overhead. Estonian émigrés have traditionally done well abroad, particularly in more classless societies such as Australia and the USA. In the early post-Soviet era, Estonia was a youth-driven culture, with radical young ministers, managers, and diplomats at the helm.

Estonians, commented one foreign student, are focused and disciplined, but there is a downside: repression, alcoholism, and a high suicide rate, particularly among men.

RESERVE

One foreign businessman, who appreciates the fact that Estonian employees are ambitious and eager to get ahead, observes: "They get the work done, but they don't tell you when it's finished; they don't communicate. Perhaps they communicate by telepathy . . !" Foreign lecturers say that Estonian students rarely interrupt their teachers or reveal their thoughts unless asked. Estonians, originally a "forest" people, and still living in a sparsely populated, densely forested land, value personal space. They reflect before offering opinions, and feedback is not freely offered. This may be due to shyness, a lack of conviction that an opinion will be appreciated, or simply reserve. However, outsiders may be surprised at the speed with which Estonians confirm friendship, moving from a cool handshake to a hug, with no lukewarm cheek-pecking in between.

Estonian Proverb
"Row quietly, and you will travel far."

BI-POLAR

According to the Estonian author Viivi Luik, there are "Summer Estonians" and "Winter Estonians." In the bleak midwinter, it gets light around noon, and dark at around 3:00 p.m.; in the bright midsummer the nights are never dark, just a haunting, lightish gray, and people become much more extroverted, partying all night and plunging naked into lakes and rivers. Some say it is the darkness and the need for a winter kick that makes coffee-drinking so popular, and the brevity of summer that sends so many households into a frenzy of cucumber-pickling and jam-making before autumn sets in. The ever-popular sauna, once a place where women went to give birth, is hugely popular in winter, not just because people still like hurling themselves into mounds of snow after a session, but for the sheer relief of stripping off heavy winter clothes.

THE GOOD LIFE

Estonians are much too puritanical to be obsessed by creature comforts. Despite the proliferation of restaurants, few people can afford to eat in them regularly, so dining out can be a rather formal experience. And the merits of gourmet cuisine are lost on some Estonian men, who will complain that dishes simply aren't big enough.

Estonians love their home space and family life. Those who can afford larger homes tend to have wooden floors (practical, in terms of winter weather), rugs, open fires, a sauna, and enough hall space for all that winter gear.

The most common way to cope with stress is to have a drink, or a sauna, or both. Estonians value their weekends, although the need to work, work, work often impinges on their free time. In the summer months, life shuts down more abruptly than in other countries, as if everyone needs a recharge to compensate for the winter gloom. Increasingly, Estonians vacation abroad; popular destinations are Norway, Egypt, and Thailand. Others retreat to the countryside, or spend time in the "summer capital," Pärnu.

CAUTIOUS OR NOT?

Despite their reputation for caution, many Estonians have huge mortgages (loan rates are low) and are, like so many people in Western cultures, living in debt. Analysts fear that the bubble may burst, plunging homeowners into negative equity, but the feel-good factor is so high, at least for those who are earning and getting along, that few people think of borrowing as risky. Savings are not high compared with other EU countries (19 percent of GDP in 2003, the lowest of the 2004 E.U. accession countries), and domestic investment is strongly reliant on foreign financing. This was highlighted as a cause for concern by the European Bank for Reconstruction and Development (2004). Although annual growth rate remains high (5.5 percent), there are concerns over regional disparities in wealth, high unemployment, rapid bank-credit growth, and high current-account deficits.

Estonians embrace novelty so long as it is useful—most noticeably cell phones, the Internet, Wi-Fi, and Skype. They tend to be conservative in moral values, but open to innovation in science and technology. They tend to view themselves as practical, excelling in applied art, such as ironwork, book illustration, ceramics, weaving, and jewelry making. At the same time, many Estonian artists, such as Raul Meel, embraced abstraction, partly as a reaction to the dictates of Soviet social realism.

A TALENT FOR DIGGING IN THEIR HEELS

During the Singing Revolution (see page 29) and the tense run-up to the restoration of independence in 1991, it was common for Estonian activists to grit their teeth and mutter, "We shall not be provoked!" In this context, it was a specific reaction to the Soviet Union, ever on the lookout for an excuse to roll in the tanks, but in other contexts also, stubbornness is seen as a virtue. The Estonian word *jonn* can mean anything from obstinacy and willfulness to endurance and tenacity. Islanders can dig their heels in even more deeply. At its noblest, *jonn* means avoiding violence; at worst, it leads to pigheadedness and an aversion to confrontation that means people will not say what they are really thinking. This can be a problem in work settings with, for example, employees simmering in silence instead of talking to the boss.

TOLERANCE

Estonians display a curious mixture of conservatism and liberalism. They are tolerant in that they do not care too much what other people do so long as it does not annoy them: what you do is your own business. During the Soviet era, Estonia was seen as a "beacon of light" by intellectuals in St. Petersburg and Moscow—a place where such "decadent" things as jazz and cabaret could be enjoyed. Estonians are not easy to shock. As one well-traveled Estonian artist comments, "I think you can ask Estonians anything. We are still quite wild people. We might tremble for a moment inside, but will usually give an honest opinion in the end."

Religion has little influence on the way people conduct their lives or judge others. Abortion is common: a fact bemoaned by those who worry about the low birthrate, but not for ethical reasons. Increasingly, women are following careers, marrying late, and delaying having children until they are confident that they have reached a career and/or financial objective. The divorce rate is one of the highest in the EU, and few would sniff at the idea of an unmarried couple living together. When discussing subjects such as euthanasia, which is currently illegal, the typical Estonian response will favor individuals being free to do as they like.

At the same time, many people, especially those above the age of thirty-five, can be old-fashioned, even provincial, in outlook. They may be suspicious of immigrants and of those who are not white; they may still connect homosexuality with pedophilia; and they may find it difficult to talk about lesbians. Some of this may be a legacy of homophobic Soviet society, when homosexuality was punishable by jail (it was legalized in 1992), but it is also a question of not having been tested. As one Australian-born Estonian commented: "Being gay is not an issue; you don't really see gay people, so you don't have to tolerate them. Estonians haven't had to spend much time thinking about people who are different from them." Many gays still conceal their sexual orientation for fear that it will compromise their jobs, and there have been reports of verbal abuse, although nothing on a par with antigay abuse in Catholic Poland, for example. There is no legal provision for gay marriage, and gays cannot adopt children. Gay activists, who launched Estonia's first annual pride parade in 2004, were disappointed when the government, in tune with public opinion, refused to legalize same-sex marriage in its new marriage law (2006). To date, the Social Democratic Party is the only political party to support gay marriage. The age of consent is fourteen, as for heterosexuals. There is a sprinkling of gay clubs and cafés in Tallinn.

Prostitution, on the other hand, is not illegal, and is closely connected to human trafficking, particularly in areas such as Narva, where unemployment is high. Such was the demand for prostitutes during the 2006 World Cup in Germany that women were trafficked in from the Baltic States, as well as from other former Soviet countries. One Estonian MEP has called for the country to follow the example of Sweden, where those who buy sex may now be penalized. But prostitution is big business, and there has been a lack of political will to address the issue.

A LUTHERAN HERITAGE

Estonians are not fundamentally a religious people. Religion has almost always been imposed by foreigners (initially by the German Order of the Knights of the Sword). There was an upsurge in religious activity following the collapse of the Soviet Union, when religious affiliation was suddenly possible, but much of this was only temporary. The essentially Lutheran heritage has, however, contributed to the Estonian work ethic. Most Estonians are hardworking, if not workaholic. You are more likely to find ardent believers among the Russian-speaking population, hence the current religious makeup of the country: Evangelical Lutheran (13.6 percent), Orthodox (12.8 percent), and Methodist, Seventh-Day Adventist, Roman Catholic, and Pentecostal (1.4 percent). Curiously, the small island of Kihnu is predominantly Orthodox, a legacy of the nineteenth century, when the Orthodox Church offered land to those who would join the Church. Only 6 percent of Estonians say they have no religion at all: if not actively religious, they are reluctant to say they do not believe in God.

Baptism and confirmation are popular, and more common than Church marriages. The traditional three-day country wedding is now more or less obsolete. A typical wedding will be a civil ceremony, followed by a party at home or at a rented venue. There is no official state religion, and Churches have little influence on politics, business, education, or intellectual life.

MULTICULTURAL ESTONIA?

Estonia cannot be described as "multicultural." If anything it is, in ethnic terms, bi-cultural (70 percent Estonian and 25 percent Russian). A sizeable portion of the population is pro-Russian, rather than pro-European, which can be a source of tension, particularly during elections. There are smaller groups of Ukrainians, Belarusians, and Finns. Since accession to the EU, there is a growing European expatriate population, while many Estonians have sought work in other EU countries, notably Finland. Some fear a brain drain, with builders, dentists, and doctors in particular seeking higher salaries abroad. Tallinn has always been, and still is, by far the most "multicultural" city in Estonia. Racism is not common, although anti-Russian sentiment, most frequently voiced by those over thirty-five, may strike outsiders as offensive.

MEN AND WOMEN

Officially, there is equality in Estonia. Suffrage and the right to run for election are universal, and have been since 1918, though interrupted by the Nazi and Soviet occupations. Twenty of the 101 members of the Riigikogu (Parliament) are women, and women make up around 30 percent of those elected to local government assemblies (2005). There are three female cabinet ministers, and three of the country's MEPs are women. The number of women in management stands at 38 percent, and is growing. Seventy percent of graduates are women; many male students drop out due to the pressure to earn money or own a status symbol such as a car. Many foreign investors appreciate the generally good language skills of Estonian women.

The government opened a gender-equality office in September 2005. When polled, Estonians tend to approve of equality and legislation to support it, but often express sexist opinions. According to the Open Estonia Foundation for the promotion of a civil society, a 2004 poll revealed that 83 percent of women and 76 percent of men believed women hold a "lesser position" in society and that, although there is a strong belief in equal opportunities, 75 percent of those questioned believed women did not make good leaders because they are "too emotional." The same percentage, however, supports legislation to promote gender equality. Although women are entitled to equal pay, this is rarely the reality. Despite their generally higher educational level, women earn roughly 75 percent of what their male counterparts earn.

Following the collapse of the Soviet Union, in which every woman, mother or not, was supposed to work, many reacted by preferring to stay at home whenever possible. This trend has been reversed, thanks to rising prices, the need to pay mortgages, and the desire for a career. There are generous paternity and maternity provisions, driven by the need to promote a higher birthrate. The father has the right to two weeks' leave during the pregnancy, the birth period, or within the two months following the birth. The parent who takes full parental leave receives benefit based on previous earnings. These provisions have been criticized for encouraging women to stay at home because their salaries tend to be lower—a tendency fueled by the shortage of affordable day care for children below the age of three.

Most working women do all or most of the domestic chores and child care (though not always the cooking), but rarely complain about this. Public opinion in this respect is conservative.

"You are lucky if your husband does anything at all," comments one Australian-born Estonian. Another reason for this is the historical absence of so many men due to war and deportation, and consequent ill health (or death), which has led to the emergence of the *perenaine* (family woman, or boss), a figure who both works and runs the home. Despite their unequal position in society, women are hardheaded and independent-minded, as well as beauty-conscious. Casual sexism is not common, but gender stereotyping is. For men, this means pressure to succeed and a tendency to pour all their energy into work, to the detriment of their emotional and physical health.

Domestic violence is, according to NGOs, a cause for concern; they claim that one in five women suffered physical, sexual, or emotional abuse in 2005. Sexual harassment is illegal, but is not considered a serious problem.

First-time visitors to Estonia will probably be struck by the generally different behavior of the sexes. Women tend to be more sociable and relaxed. Men are much more taciturn, though likely to open up after a few drinks—whereupon their interlocutor may be subjected to a marathon monologue. Such initial reticence was neatly illustrated during an interview in London with the Estonian composer Veljo Tormis. Following a long, comprehensive, and thoroughly researched question from a British journalist, Tormis was silent, then replied: "You've said it all," instead of offering a response.

ATTITUDES TO FOREIGNERS

Attitudes to foreigners, in particular those from the West, are generally positive, although there is a love-hate relationship with the neighboring Finns. There is a clichéd image of the latter as loud and drunken (alcohol is much cheaper in Estonia than in Finland). There are strong cultural and commercial ties between the two countries, however, and there is an Estonian saying that "Every Estonian has [knows] a Finn." Well-educated Russians from Russia are also generally welcome. Tallinn is a popular destination for Russian tourists throughout the year, but especially on New Year's Eve. English-speaking foreigners are generally very welcome, although there has been criticism of British stag-party antics. Estonia is still grateful for British naval aid during the Independence War, commemorated by a plaque outside the Maritime Museum in Tallinn. Many Estonians are now well traveled, particularly with the growing number of no-frills flights to and from Tallinn. Western European, rather than Eastern European, destinations are generally favored.

HUMOR: PAINT IT BLACK

Estonians are quick to laugh at themselves. Sometimes it's hard to fathom the joke, so deadpan is the face and so obscure or wry the sentiment. Humor is often ironic and mocking, highlighting what is bleak, absurd, or surreal. This partly

explains the continuing wealth of animated films, a
subversive industry that survived the transition to
capitalism. Many writers, too, favor fantastical and
surreal situations, among them Mati Unt, Arvo
Valton, and Meehis Heinsaar. Nobel Prize nominee
Jaan Kross illustrates cruel moments of history with
a humanizing sense of absurdity. In general,
Estonian humor is sophisticated and dark, cerebral
rather than ribald. As in Estonian folklore, laughs
are often at the expense of the wealthy, powerful, or
pompous, and in favor of quick-witted, down-to-
earth underlings. Vanity and current affairs are
always good targets. In the first years of restored
independence, people would ask, "Why do we need
so many banks? Because we are so poor," and
"Why do we need so many beauty salons? Because
we are so ugly."

IS THERE A NATIONAL IDENTITY?

There is a strong sense of national identity, which
comes to the fore in sporting competitions. When
Estonia unexpectedly won the Eurovision Song
Contest in 2000, there was much dancing
on tables in Estonian
embassies across the world,
and jubilation that this would
help put the country on the
map. To some extent, Estonian
national identity is relatively
young, growing out of the
period of "National Awakening"

in the nineteenth century and sealed by the creation of the national epic, *Kalevipoeg* (see page 20), a tale that celebrates Estonian *jonn* (page 59).

The most important representatives of the country abroad are cultural figures, among them the composer Arvo Pärt; conductors Eri Klas and Neeme and Paavo Järvi; author Jaan Kross; poet Jaan Kaplinski; animation director Priit Pärn; and ballet dancers Agnes Oaks and Thomas Edur, the darlings of English National Ballet. The emergence of supermodel Carmen Kass sealed the image of Estonian women as beautiful, and led to an explosion of modeling agencies in Tallinn.

Regional identity is also strong. Semi-mock rivalry between Tallinn and Tartu continues to thrive. People enjoy returning to their hometown; those from Pärnu, for example, go back there whenever possible for a dose of sea air. People from the south are proud of their "hilly" landscape. Those from Võru, near the Latvian border, have a distinctive accent, almost a dialect. Estonians are strongly individualistic, but are ultimately aware of the need to stick together, particular in tough times.

National identity is first and foremost centered on the language, a Finno-Ugric tongue that supposedly won an international competition for the most beautiful language with the phrase *Sõida tasa üle silla* ("Cross the bridge quietly"). It is a thoroughly Estonian piece of advice.

chapter three

FESTIVALS & CELEBRATIONS

In a country historically apprehensive about its survival, festive folk traditions are still revered. While many of the most treasured indigenous customs have a Christian veneer, they are pagan in origin, and linked to events such as seasonal change—midsummer, for example, or the beginning of winter. Music, in particular song, plays an important part in these rituals. Other more recent celebrations, like the national Song Festival, are both cultural and political in origin. Estonian celebrations tend to be low-key and dignified rather than wild and boisterous. Traditional dances are slow, even plodding.

Estonia's internationally acclaimed music festivals celebrate everything from classical and contemporary music to folk, bagpipes, and organs, which are of high quality, especially in the churches of Tallinn. The international winter film festival in Tallinn also draws spectators from abroad. Some of the country's newest events are more tourist-oriented, such as Tallinn's Old Town Days.

The number of obligatory national flag days, introduced after the restoration of independence, was recently reduced to what many considered a more "sensible" total of three. It is no longer required for institutions to raise the flag on September 1, the Day of Knowledge, although many still do—an illustration of the deep-seated respect for self-improvement. Most of the remaining flag days are related to Estonia's self-determination and are reflective commemorations rather than celebrations—another reminder that history is still very much remembered.

PUBLIC HOLIDAYS

Ten public holidays are observed nationwide. Schools, banks, government offices, museums, and most businesses close on these days. Most cinemas and many restaurants remain open. If the day falls on a Sunday, the following Monday is taken as a holiday. There are also several regional and local holidays.

January 1: New Year's Day
February 24: Independence Day (1918)
March/April: Good Friday
May 1: Spring Day
Seventh Monday after Easter: Pentecost
June 23: Victory Day
June 24: St. John's Day or Midsummer Day
August 20: Day of Restoration of Independence
December 25: Christmas Day
December 26: Boxing Day

NATIONAL DAYS (NOT PUBLIC HOLIDAYS)
February 2: Anniversary of the Tartu Peace Treaty
March 14: Native Language Day
May 14: Mothers' Day
June 4: National Flag Day
June 14: Day of Mourning and Commemoration
November 2: All Souls' Day
November 12: Fathers' Day
November 16: Day of Declaration of Sovereignty

For information about any special events to be held during your visit, contact local tourist offices or visit www.visitestonia.com, www.tourism.ee, or Estonian embassy Web sites.

A FESTIVE CALENDAR
February
As the winter days lighten, the cultural calendar begins in Tallinn with the Baroque Music Days, a weeklong celebration of early music run by the city's leading early music specialists. Concerts are also staged in other cities, among them Tartu.

Independence Day, on February 24, marks the anniversary of the proclamation of the Independence Manifesto in 1918 that led to the founding of the Republic of Estonia. A modest military parade takes place on Vabaduse väljak and the atmosphere is one of quiet restraint; following the proclamation, it took Estonian soldiers and ill-equipped volunteers nearly two years to clear the territory of German and Soviet Russian forces.

On Fat (Shrove) Tuesday (*Vastapäev*) the tradition is to go sledding and skiing. Traditional food is not pancakes but bean or pea soup with pig's feet, and buns filled with cream.

April

Some people, but by no means everyone, mark April Fool's Day (*Esimene Aprill*) with pranks. Newspapers often run spoof items.

Easter (*Lihavõtted)*, aside from its religious meaning, is generally welcomed as a festival marking the end of a long, dark winter. The only official holiday of the Easter season is Easter Sunday. Easter is also described as a Spring, Eggs, Meat (in connection with Lent), or Swing holiday, the last of these being linked to the custom of swinging on large wooden swings on Easter Sunday. Good Friday is a quiet day, and everyone is back to work or school on Easter Monday. Easter Sunday is a family affair, with relatives getting together for long lunches. One popular traditional dish is *pashka*, or *pasha*, a Russian-style dessert made with curd cheese, almonds, and raisins. In the run-up to Easter people seek out the whitest eggs for painting, and many hold egg-painting parties. The eggs are used to decorate the table. Children play at breaking eggs, as in British conker competitions. It is also customary to bring young willow twigs indoors for sprouting; sometimes grass seeds are planted in pots.

Easter, according to recent polls, is most respected by the older generation, by women, and by non-Estonians (including Russian-speakers and followers of the Orthodox faith). Rural Easter customs, such as games involving eggs, are usually enacted at the Estonian Open Air Museum. One in five Estonians attends a Church service. Note that Russian Orthodox Easter is held approximately two weeks later. In Tallinn, be sure to catch the sound of the booming bells at St. Nicholas Church, on Vene Street. This holiday is increasingly commercial; compared with other European cities, however, shops show restraint.

In late April, the Jazzkaar festival sees jazz, blues, and world-music concerts across the country, with local talent bolstered by big international acts.

May

May 1 is Spring Day and is, as in Finland, mainly celebrated by students partying; it could be better described as "Youth Day."

Tallinn celebrates its City Day on May 15, in memory of the Danish king granting the city the rights of Lübeck in 1248, which paved the way for its accession to the Hanseatic League.

Pärnu hosts a triennial International Choir Contest in late May (to be held next in 2010).

June

During the first week of June, Tallinn hosts the Old Town Days, an attempt to re-create the city's medieval atmosphere, with jousting, minstrels, traditional Estonian music, and open-air markets.

June 14 is a day of mourning that commemorates the first mass deportation from the Baltic States under Stalin, in 1941.

June 23, Victory Day, is a public holiday and a day of official ceremonies commemorating a decisive moment in the country's Independence War of 1918–20. On this day in 1919, Estonian forces defeated the Germans in the northern Latvian town of Cesis, putting an end to their attempts to regain control of the region. It has come to symbolize all Estonian attempts to regain and retain independence, which is why, during the Soviet occupation, bonfires were lit on the eve of St. John's Day, or midsummer, on June 24. One pre-Soviet tradition has been restored: the Estonian president lights a fire on the morning of June 23, so that a flame of independence can be lit and used to light bonfires across the country.

St. John's Day is a pagan festival (the Crusaders gave it the saint's name), held shortly after the longest day in the year. It marked the end of spring sowing and a rest from farming work until haymaking. In his Chronicle of the Province of Livonia, the sixteenth-century writer Balthasar Rüssow berated Estonians for celebrating pagan rituals on St. John's Day and for lighting fires, leaping over the flames, and indulging in drinking, singing, and dancing instead of showing enthusiasm for Church. Originally, lighting and leaping over a fire was supposed to guarantee prosperity, a good harvest, and general good luck; it was also believed to reduce the risk of a fire burning down one's home. Midsummer is also steeped in romance. According to legend, the lovers Koit (dawn) and Hämark (dusk) meet only once, on the shortest night of the year, when they may briefly kiss. Earthly mortals, meanwhile, hunt for fern flowers that supposedly bloom only at midsummer.

Today, many people leave the towns and cities and head out to the countryside to celebrate St. John's Eve with friends or family. Sometimes it is a quiet event, with everyone sitting around the fire, gazing into the flames; at others it is a party, with a barbecue, dancing, singing, and drinking.

Late June marks the beginning of Pärnu's stint as "summer capital" and the opening of the prestigious David Oistrakh Festival, named after the Russian violinist who often visited the seaside town. The festival traditionally features master classes by Neeme Järvi, and continues until mid-July.

July
Every four to five years, Tallinn hosts the Estonian Song Festival, an extraordinary event at which as many as twenty-five thousand choral singers, and crowds of up to three hundred thousand, gather on the vast stage of the Song Bowl grounds, overlooking the Bay of Tallinn. It begins with a colorful procession through the capital, with choirs from across the country and abroad wearing folk,

regional, and national dress. When prohibited songs were sung during the 1988 Song Festival, held under the Soviet occupation (the Russians "controlled" the festival via the introduction of patriotic Soviet songs), this helped to spark the so-called Singing Revolution, which culminated with the restoration of independence. The next festival is scheduled for 2009.

Every year in early July, the song festival grounds stage the five-day Öllesummer (Beer Summer), with pop, folk, jazz, world, and classical concerts providing an excuse for locals and tourists to  down substantial quantities of Estonian ale.

In July in Pärnu, the International Documentary and Anthropology Film Festival attracts a crowd rather higher of brow, and showcases films for children.

Organ soloists from around the world take part in Tallinn's International Organ Festival, performing in historic churches throughout the capital in July and August.

August

The public holiday on August 20 celebrates the restoration of independence in 1991, when the failed hard-line coup in Moscow led to the collapse of the Soviet Union. Museums are usually closed on this day. In late August, Tallinn hosts the August

Dance Festival, a showcase for the latest trends in contemporary dance, held at the atmospheric Kanuti Guildi Saal.

The seaside season ends during the last week of August, when people light candles along the seashore, as if mourning the passing of summer.

November

All Souls' Day (*Hingedepäev*), November 2, a time of prayer for the departed, acquired particular poignancy during the Soviet occupation, when people visited the graves of friends and relatives, often remembering the atrocities suffered by so many during war and deportation. It was not a day sanctioned by the Soviet Union, so visits were often made surreptitiously. At night, one could usually determine whether households were Estonian- or Russian-speaking because All Souls candles burned only in the windows of the former. This deep-seated reverence for the dead and for respecting and maintaining graves predates the Christian era.

Martinma (*Mardipäev*), on November 11, marks the end of All Souls. A blend of Western European and Balto-Finnic customs, it signals the end of the agrarian year and the coming of winter, and is especially popular in rural areas. Children visit houses on St. Martin's Eve, singing Martinmas songs and offering good luck for crops and households. Traditional dishes include goose (for the better-off), blood pudding, chicken, pork, and lamb. St Martin's Day is celebrated with games, concerts, and dancing. St. Catherine's Day

(*Kadripäev*) also marks the coming of winter. It is similar to St. Martin's, in that beggars (*kadris*) traditionally went from house to house asking for gifts in return for blessings and songs. As the festival is associated with a female saint, men dress up in women's clothes, wearing light colors as a symbol of the coming snow. As women traditionally tended the sheep, many of the folk songs associated with this event offer good luck to flocks.

The most important cultural festival in the run-up to Christmas is the two-week Black Nights film festival, which begins in late November and offers new feature films from around the world, competitions for student films, films for children, and animated shorts. Christmas Jazz, an offshoot of Jazzkaar, takes place at around the same time.

December

Every two years, toward the end of the year, Tallinn hosts Midwinter Night's Dream, an international avant-garde theater festival, next scheduled for 2008.

The Christmas (*Jõulud*) period begins with Advent, when a German-style Christmas market is held in the Town Hall Square. Stalls sell farm produce and Christmas cookies, knitted and woven clothes and textiles, and jewelry. Fairgoers warm themselves with punch and eat roast suckling pig, and children visit Santa's grotto. According to local folklore, the first public Christmas tree was raised in Tallinn's Town Hall Square in 1441. In the run-up to Christmas, the Estonian Open Air Museum hosts Christmas concerts and traditional games.

Although Christmas as an official holiday was cancelled during the Soviet occupation, Estonians continued to celebrate quietly at home, some even attending Church services on Christmas Eve. As in Scandinavia, the focal point is Christmas Eve, when traditional meals are enjoyed and presents opened—though traditionally children cannot receive presents until they have recited a poem. This is a private, family occasion, sometimes not even including the extended family.

The Estonian for Christmas, *Jõulud,* is a pre-Christian word (*Jul* in Swedish, *Yule* in English). This pagan celebration was linked to the sun's "birthday" and the winter solstice, and looked forward to an increase in daylight.

Eating as much as possible on Christmas Eve was supposed to ensure plenty of food throughout the coming year; men would eat seven times to give them the strength of seven men. Pork, sauerkraut, blood sausages, baked potatoes, beetroot, and gingerbread were left out all night for visiting ancestors and spirits; fires stayed alight throughout the night. Stars and frost were used to predict the weather and harvest for the coming year, while straw was brought inside for children to play with. Beer and mead were brewed on December 21, in sufficient quantities to last until the end of the holiday on January 6.

New Yea (*Uusaasta)* in Tallinn attracts mainly Russian and Finnish tourists. Bars, nightclubs, and restaurants hold parties and dinners, and if you plan to go out be sure to book in advance, even if you're planning to spend an evening in one of the city's pubs. Toward midnight, a crowd gathers in Town Hall Square for fireworks and champagne. Every year, the Estonian National Opera holds a New Year's Eve ball, an evening of dance and operetta that begins with a waltz and features a different theme each year. There are several bars, and ball goers can dine in the Winter Garden. New Year's Day is extremely quiet.

WEDDINGS AND OTHER RITES OF PASSAGE

Church weddings are not especially popular. In the prewar republic, it was common to be married by a pastor in your own home, and to have a party there afterward. Today, those who can afford it tend to choose a civil ceremony with a party in a restaurant or rented venue. For many young couples whose parents cannot help financially, this means saving for months, if not years. If you are invited to a wedding, you should acknowledge the invitation as soon as possible, and you should take a present. There may be a gift registry to help you decide what to give.

Back in the nineteenth century, things were very different. Before the bride left her parents' house, she would be taken to the sauna. She would then go to the bridegroom's house. Traditionally, the wedding party on the following day marked the moment when the bride was properly married, with the ceremony taking place during the party itself. She was "married" when she donned a decorative headdress; after a festive dance, the young couple retired together. The third day was mainly devoted to giving and receiving presents and to the establishment of good relations between the two families. Parties and games sometimes continued in the homes of both bride and groom the following day. It was considered bad luck to marry during an old moon.

Although Estonians are not enthusiastic churchgoers (Orthodox Russian-speaking Estonians tend to be more devout), baptism in church is quite popular. If you are invited to attend a baptism, take a gift—perhaps an item of silver. If you are to be a godparent, an engraved silver spoon would be appropriate. Traditionally, children were often given the names of their grandparents. Baptisms could take place at home or in church. Festive feasting, often continuing for more than a day, used to take place after a baptism; today it is usual to have a more modest party, with a meal in the family home.

One of the most expensive social obligations for parents these days is the ritual "coming of age" party, which occurs when children graduate from school, and is often combined with confirmation. Meeting the expense of these occasions is a challenge for many families. If you are a relative or close family friend, it is customary to take flowers to the party and to offer money. Students generally give flowers to their class teachers on the last day of school.

As a general rule, if you are invited to a baptism or confirmation party, you should acknowledge an invitation with the same degree of formality with which it was issued, and bring a gift.

Funerals

Funerals usually take place within four or five days of the death. The relatives generally put an announcement in the local newspaper. Traditionally, the body was laid out at home in a coffin for friends and family to view before burial, and this still often happens in rural areas; otherwise the coffin may be open for viewing in the chapel where the funeral is to be held. It was traditional for a box of earth to be set aside, and mourners invited to throw some into the grave. Increasingly now, however, people are requesting cremation.

Anyone can attend a burial or cremation, but will not necessarily be invited to the social event that follows. Post-funeral gatherings are, at least initially, quiet and low-key, and held at the home of a friend or relative, or in a restaurant or church hall. The rich may choose to show off their wealth, for example by booking grand funeral cars. Russian cultural tradition favors noisier wakes, sometimes in the form of a graveside "party," and longer periods of mourning. It is customary to look after graves well and to place candles on birthdays, on other important anniversaries, and, above all, at All Souls.

chapter four

MAKING FRIENDS

In the social sphere, you could describe Estonians as polite and plain speaking, but reserved to a point that might, at a first meeting, appear cold, or even rude. They are much more reserved than most North American or British people, but when they come out of their shells they are generally direct, and mean what they say. Younger, more traveled, and more cosmopolitan people tend to be less formal in their social relations. Most Estonians, however, will be kind and helpful as long as you respect their private space and do not try to rush them, although they can also be unexpectedly spontaneous.

A sense of humor is usually much appreciated and helps to break the ice, particularly if you show that you can laugh at yourself.

Any effort to speak Estonian also goes down well. It is important, once again, to point out that there is a gaping difference between Estonians and "Russian-speakers," the latter generally being Slavic and more outgoing. Estonians will tell you that such warmth does not necessarily lead to more authentic or loyal friendships, and that an Estonian friend is a friend for life.

Estonians set great store by privacy, especially in their home life, and most of your social contacts with Estonians will be in public places. Although there is a growing moneyed class who may be only too happy to show you their spacious homes, most people still live in smallish flats, and may be reluctant to invite you there in case they are judged "poor." Home tends to be the preserve of family life, and invitations out to cultural events may therefore be more common.

HOW NOT TO BE AN EXPATRIATE

Relations with colleagues may initially be formal, but can quickly develop into a more friendly rapport if you get on well. Indeed, your most likely way into Estonian life is through working relationships or, if you are a parent, through nurseries or schools. Working relationships, however, do not easily extend to people's private lives. Says one Estonian artist who has spent several years living outside Estonia, "One can work together and meet for years, yet never be invited to someone's house." Both Estonians and Russian-speaking Estonians are more bound to their families and extended families than many people in Western Europe. Although the younger, more traveled generations are often more open, they still tend to have families at a younger age than on average in the West, and the family circle remains fairly closed. Estonians with experience of living abroad often say they find it easier, on their return, to befriend foreigners living in Estonia. The same Estonian artist observes that Estonians can be "non-talkative to the point of seeming rude." This can extend to people not bothering to reply to invitations or turn up to an event you have organized. In such situations, it is acceptable to inquire and even nag.

To immerse yourself in Estonian life and culture, try to get out of Tallinn and visit rural areas (although fewer people will speak English). People tend to be more friendly and welcoming outside the big towns. You can explore the country's Russian-speaking culture, which would mean visiting towns like Narva, or frequenting cafés and bars that are more "Russian." Estonians and Russian-speakers often go to pubs popular with expats because they are curious to meet non-Estonians.

There is obviously not a long history of expatriate life in Estonia, although the community is growing. There is, for example, an International Women's Club. The monthly English-language magazine, *City Paper*, which covers all three Baltic States, and the *In Your Pocket* city guides to Tallinn, Tartu, and Pärnu give useful information about culture and entertainment. For information about expat baby groups or clubs, it is best to contact your local embassy in Tallinn. The U.S. and British embassies' Web sites include news of forthcoming cultural and other events.

BEING A FOREIGN STUDENT
Estonian universities set out to attract international
students. They organize English-language study
programs and want to make the lives of visiting
foreign students as enjoyable as possible. These
students consequently feel welcome, and
find it easy to make friends. The
Universities of Tallinn and Tartu have
numerous student societies and participate
in exchange programs with other European
universities. Most of the foreign students at
the University of Tartu, which has a long-
standing exchange agreement with the
University of Toronto, are from Finland,
Sweden, Latvia, Russia, the United States, or
Germany. Attractions include the high quality of
tuition and the relatively low cost of studying and
living in Estonia.

CLUBS, CLASSES, AND COMMUNITIES
Estonians are not generally enthusiastic about
clubs or amateur groups. Even people who get
together to pursue common interests rarely meet
outside the shared activity. Sporting activities,
however, are popular, and can be a good way to
meet locals. If you don't speak Estonian, you will
almost certainly find that some Estonians taking
part in these activities can speak reasonably good
English. One way to meet locals is to enroll in a
language course, which may be Estonian or a

foreign language. Spanish is currently popular.

Foreigners may be surprised to learn that initially befriending a member of the Russian-speaking or Estonian-speaking community almost inevitably locks you into that community, such is the gap between the two. Even clubs, bars, and cafés may be identified as places where either Estonians or Russians go. In general, however, Russian-speakers tend to be more open, sociable, and lively. There is also a significant cultural difference between non-Soviet Russians who lived in Russian areas during the first Estonian Republic, for example in the villages near Lake Peipsi, and those who moved to Estonia during the Soviet era, and who mostly live in industrial areas.

HANGING OUT

Estonians, in particular the men, tend to be enthusiastic drinkers, and open up after a glass or two, so pubs, clubs, and bars are good places to try to meet them. Steer clear of the obvious tourist hangouts, especially beyond the Old Town, and you'll find plenty of locals enjoying a few drinks. There's a lively young club scene in both Tallinn and Tartu (during the academic year, at least), and most bars are open until the early hours. In summer, Estonians flock to Pärnu for sun, sand, and spa treatments, and tend to be less inhibited during their beachside sojourns.

HOSPITALITY

There are few rules about visiting Estonians in their home, apart from the fact that most people don't wear shoes indoors, and will expect the same from you. Make sure your socks are presentable!

Formal dinner parties are not common and, although cookbooks are becoming increasingly popular, Estonians in general are not gourmets. You are more likely to be invited either to a party—without food, but perhaps with nibbles— or to "tea," which usually means coffee and cake. Reply to an invitation with the same degree of formality with which it is offered: an e-mail response to an e-mail invitation is fine.

If a colleague does invite you home to dinner, this could be anything from a formal to a very relaxed event. It is, however, almost always a sign of friendship.

If you want to return the compliment of a dinner party, but are not living in Estonia, it is perfectly acceptable to invite people to dinner in a restaurant or to a cultural evening, for instance at the opera or ballet. If you are a resident, and are hosting a dinner party of your own, you can set the level of formality. Estonian guests tend to be adaptable, or even to assume that you know best.

In general, Estonians will not expect you to know how they go about things and will therefore be tolerant of any perceived gaffes.

Dress

For social occasions, including visits to people's homes, the "smart casual" dress code is usually appropriate, with an emphasis on the "smart." Estonians, in particular men, tend to dress conservatively. Wealthier people may be acutely conscious of labels, but this does not mean you have to be the same. Women tend to be more dress-conscious, formal, and stylish, and beauty salons are very "in" these days. Many Estonian women dress formally for social events, including trips to the theater or a concert. Nobody, however, will laugh at you for dressing more casually.

Gift Giving

In the event that you are invited into an Estonian home, take a gift with you, such as wine, chocolates, or flowers. It is traditional to take a *torte* (cake) to a housewarming. When offering flowers, present them unwrapped, and don't give white flowers, which are associated with funerals. You should, ideally, present an odd number of flowers; even numbers are also associated with funerals (though few Estonians would expect a foreigner to know this). It is common to take a single flower to a party or for an event such as an exhibition opening or a book launch.

Gifts may or may not be opened in front of the giver, so, if you are the recipient, you won't be at fault for doing either.

> ### *POINTS OF ETIQUETTE*
> - Always offer to remove your shoes on entering someone's home. Older people may bring their own slippers, and younger people usually pad around in socks or tights.
> - Be sincere: Estonians are quick to detect lack of authenticity.
> - Eat what you can and compliment the host on anything homemade that you enjoy.
> - If your hosts are drinking alcohol, join in, even if only for a small glass. Estonian men, in particular, may see drinking as bonding. It is common to say "*Prozit*" or "*Terviseks*."
> - Don't be offended if someone fails to return an invitation to dinner: it may be that their home is smaller than yours and they feel uncomfortable about this.
> - Lunch, especially on nonworking days, tends to be between 3:00 and 5:00 p.m. and to be the major meal of the day.

THE SAUNA

If you are invited to a sauna, you will almost certainly be expected to sit in the sauna naked. Don't be alarmed. In public swimming pools, there are usually separate saunas, or separate days, for men and women. Locals will be surprised if you respond bashfully to this custom. If you are having a sauna in a private home, or at a private party in a public swimming pool, sauna, or spa, a discreet system is in place: men usually enter the sauna separately (not necessarily before the women) and plunge into the small pool (or cold plunge pool) naked. The rest of the company is not expected to take much notice of this, and certainly not to stare. The sauna goers then put on their towels or bathrobes and join the rest of the company. Similarly, women will visit the sauna as a separate group and follow the same routine; men will be expected to ignore their nudity. Estonians, for all their modesty, are at ease being naked. Children are also welcome. (In public saunas they would expect to be sexually segregated from the official school-going age of seven). If attending a private sauna with friends or at a party, you may find yourself being beaten on the back with wet birch twigs by another member of the party. This is said to be good for the circulation. You will be expected to return the favor.

CONVERSATIONAL DOS AND DONT'S

- As with so many things in Estonia, a country that has changed dramatically in the last fifteen years, there are few rules about what you can and can't say. As a general rule, it is good to follow your host. If someone asks you what you do, or earn, you can ask the same. In general, it is perfectly acceptable to ask, "And what do you do?"
- Estonians do not talk too much about themselves, although some may want to tell you about their work, especially if they view

themselves as successful. Be modest about your own work, earnings, and property.

- It is perfectly acceptable to talk about business matters at social occasions—remember there is a strong Lutheran work ethic—and to ask questions about Estonian politics, history, religion, or attitudes to the European Union.

- Be sensitive about relations between the Russian-speaking and Estonian-speaking communities. It is fine to ask how the communities interact, but if you suggest that Estonia is "abusing" the rights of Russians, you could cause deep offense and risk a heated argument. Apply the same sensitivity to discussions about the Nazi occupation or perceived "neo-Nazism" today.

- Estonians will happily talk about Estonian nature, culture, history, and language, and about Estonian sporting exploits.

- Show respect for the historical sufferings of the Estonian people.

Thanks

It is not necessary to send handwritten thanks after receiving hospitality, although these would be appreciated. Estonia is so e-mail oriented that electronic thanks are perfectly acceptable, as long as they are sent as soon as possible after the event. You may also telephone or text to thank people.

chapter five

DAILY LIFE

QUALITY OF LIFE

Estonia is a largely rural country. The most prosperous area, and where the vast majority of wealth is concentrated, is Tallinn and its suburbs. The accommodation costs in the capital have soared, forcing out some of the less well-off and unemployed. The poorest regions of the country are the northeast, in particular Ida-Virumaa, and rural areas.

The social welfare network today aims to provide universal social support and security, with a focus on improved social equilibrium, but it is something of a work in progress. The more "enlightened" members of Estonian society often say that they do not believe the welfare system offers enough protection to those who are economically or socially underprivileged. One art historian with extensive experience of living outside Estonia commented that: "There is a media-generated opinion that such people are usually 'guilty,' and that the state should not 'nanny' people." Pensions and health care are financed from social tax (33 percent of the gross payroll: 20 percent for pensions and 13 percent for health insurance), which is paid by all employers and the self-employed. Other benefits are financed from the state budget and local taxes. Unemployment benefit and sick leave are low, although the latter has improved.

Concern about the low birthrate has led to a generous parental benefit. Introduced in 2004, this guarantees a percentage of salary for up to a year for the parent who stays at home. This is based on the salary of the preceding calendar year. As most eligible parents are young women in their early careers, the benefit may be much lower than if calculated according to current salary. The maximum benefit is 19,245 EEK per month. This ceiling has been criticized because, statistically, men earn more than women, so women may feel obliged to stay at home. Child benefit decreases with time, and is just 313 EEK per month for a fifteen-year-old. Given the lack of affordable care for children under the age of three, the tendency, again, is for women to give up work.

There is some realization, especially in relation to health care, that the current provision cannot continue; but it would be a brave politician who suggested increasing the tax burden to sustain it.

Although employment soared between 1995 and 2005, and there is a shortage of labor, not everyone is doing well. Many families live in small or shared accommodation. Although Estonia has one of the highest rates of home ownership of the EU's 2004 intake, many people struggle to pay rent. It is still common to find grandparents living with their children and their families.

HEALTH CARE

The health-care system, based on the principle of solidarity and therefore universal, is in good shape. Doctors and nurses are well educated; equipment, given the post-Soviet overhaul, is modern; and standards of hygiene are high. Emergency treatment is usually prompt and good.

There is concern about the number of doctors and nurses who have sought better-paid work abroad since Estonia joined the EU. The population as a whole is in better health than during the Soviet occupation, thanks to better diets and medical care, but work-related stress and alcoholism are problems, particularly for men.

There is still a fondness for natural self-help remedies such as by-products of honey, sea-buckthorn juice, to boost the immune system, and aronia (chokeberry), for high blood pressure. Estonians tend to be stoical, and rarely complain about their health.

FAMILY LIFE

The family is very much the center of social life in Estonia, and the ideal of a nuclear family is strong. Close family members are usually regularly in touch, while respecting each other's space. Depending on proximity, people visit parents and in-laws once or twice a week, and do not generally see this as an obligation. There is some truth to the generalization that Estonian mothers-in-law are relatively undemanding compared with those in other cultures, including Russian culture, but grandmothers tend to provide a great deal of child care. Most families still go out of their way to ensure that grandparents, no matter how old or disabled, can stay at home or with their families. To outsiders, family relations can seem cool, but this is deceptive.

Some Estonian commentators claim that life since the restoration of independence has become more selfish, and that people are now more likely to neglect their relatives, possibly because of heavy work commitments.

Children

Estonian society is child friendly, but in a matter-of-fact rather than a sentimental way. In general, children are treated with respect and are welcome at concert venues and in restaurants and cafés (until 9:00 p.m.), as long as they are not out of control. There is, however, a lack of ramps for strollers, and access to public transportation, for example trams, is not always easy. People are usually helpful, but you may have to ask.

The birthrate has been declining for more than a decade, while the number of retirees is growing. The declining birthrate is one reason the Estonian press unfairly criticizes women who put their careers before children. Despite this, there is little stigma attached to couples without children. People tend to marry later in life than they did during the

Soviet occupation, when marrying and having children could help you to obtain a bigger flat. There is a lack of affordable child care for the under-threes, hence the reliance on grandparents helping out. Parents are generally devoted, and their lives revolve around their children. Good education is a high priority. However, many Estonian men expect women to do everything in the home, even if they work full time. Mothers tend to put much more energy than fathers into parenting, although there are signs of a more equitable approach in younger couples.

Although Estonians are not, on the whole, religious believers, rituals such as baptism and first communion are quite common. One of the most important rites of passage for a child—and worryingly expensive for parents—is school graduation, which has the same significance as a twenty-first birthday in countries such as the UK.

Young Adults
As we have seen, the age of consent for both heterosexual and homosexual activity is fourteen. The legal age for voting, driving, and marrying is eighteen. Eleven months' military service is compulsory for men aged nineteen to twenty-eight.

The Third Age
Many of the poorest members of society are retirees, who live on an average monthly income of about 3,000 EEK (retirees who were deported during the Soviet era receive double the state

pension). Life expectancy for women is about seventy-eight, and for men about sixty-six, which is especially low in relation to the EU average. Lifestyle and alcohol consumption generally account for this difference.

Despite the aging population and declining birthrate, Estonia has a relatively sustainable pension system. The state pension is based on work contributions relating to social tax and the national state pension. The latter is accessible to anyone who has lived in Estonia for five years.

Nursing homes are seen as a last resort. In the aftermath of the restoration of independence, the development and regulation of special care was not a priority. As a result, many care homes are overcrowded and living conditions are often unsatisfactory. There are also significant differences in quality between the regions. One controversial issue is that special care services are not easily accessible to people who live on their own, but require some help to remain independent. The Ministry of Social Affairs has acknowledged that this needs to be improved.

EDUCATION
Education is hugely valued by most Estonians. Schooling consists of compulsory basic education (*põhikool,* from seven to sixteen) and secondary general education. The usual grading system is a five-point scale (five being excellent). The basic school-leaving certificate allows students to

continue their education for three years at a secondary general school (*gymnasium*), graduating with a certificate that gives access to higher education or a vocational institution. Although children officially begin school at the age of seven, most attend preschool, especially if both parents work.

Since the restoration of independence in 1991, there has been generous investment in school buildings and technology. There is also a greater drive for results, as life has become much more competitive. Most schools have access to the Internet, although Wi-Fi is not available in every part of the country. There are few private schools, and private education is not popular, so high is faith in the state system. The oldest school in Tallinn, Gustavus Adolphus, has the equivalent of British grammar-school status, and fees are low. There is huge competition to enter this and other selective schools, such as the French Lycée, for which there are entrance exams. In general, schools adhere to the basic national curriculum. Official state schools are directly financed by the state. State education is secular. There tends to be great emphasis on discipline, sometimes at the expense of creativity and independent thinking. English is the most popular foreign language, followed by French, German, or Russian, depending on what a school can offer.

There are several Russian-speaking schools in Tallinn. It has often been said, by both locals and outsiders, that there should be more investment in good-quality Estonian-language teaching for Russian-speakers, but that there is a lack of political will. Opponents say that those who want to learn Estonian, which is the only official language, should pay for lessons, but not all can afford to. Respecting and preserving high Russian culture via good-quality teaching in Russian while encouraging integration via good Estonian-language tuition is a delicate balance.

Higher education consists of universities (*ülikool*) and applied higher-education institutions (*rakenduskörgkool*). There are six public and twelve private universities. The academic year runs from September to June. University consists of two levels, totaling five years. The usual length for doctoral studies is four years. Higher-education institutions set quotas for foreign students, who must be eligible for university in their own country, must take entrance exams, and must have a good knowledge of Estonian, English, German, or Russian, depending on the institution. Most university courses are in Estonian, but there are academic groups in which these other languages are used.

THE HOME AND HOMEMAKING

Estonians tend to be attached to their own homes and hometowns, even if they move away for work reasons. They tend not to move often, especially once they have purchased their own home. Most people commute by car, partly because of the inefficient rail system. Homes tend to be seen as private places, as a refuge from working life and increasingly, for the better off, as a status symbol. A sea view is especially desirable. More than 80 percent of the population own their own homes, and such is the continuing building boom that many people place deposits on apartments or houses that have not yet been constructed.

Increasingly, families build their own homes, for example, on the outskirts of Tallinn, as the ideal is to have plenty of private space, a garden, and a sauna, even if this means commuting to work.

 There is still plenty of room for expansion in this sparsely populated land. Those who can afford to think about such things delight in having fashionable interiors, although there is a relatively limited range of materials. DIY is popular with men, and gardens are painstakingly tended.

Renting is more common for young people and foreign residents. The cheapest accommodation is to be found in high-rise apartment complexes built during the Soviet occupation. Although the setting can be gray, many of the apartments have been carefully renovated, and rents are significantly cheaper than in more attractive areas. Expats prefer to live in flats in Tallinn's Old Town, or in its suburbs where houses have gardens. Real-estate agencies usually charge a fee equivalent to a month's rent. Water, electricity, and heating costs are usually included in the rent, but it is advisable to check this.

The building boom in the last decade has necessitated an influx of workers from abroad, for example from Poland and Ukraine. There is, however, a shortage of social housing. With many families borrowing money at favorable mortgage rates, there are concerns about a future collapse into negative equity.

Some areas of the capital are still economically depressed, especially the Soviet-block neighborhood of Lasnamäe. Kopli, once a working-class Russian-speaking ghetto west of Tallinn, is slowly on the rise, following the neighborhood of Kalamaja, which is closer to the city and has pretty wooden houses. Property values have risen sharply since accession to the EU (18 percent in 2005.) It is common for the better-off to own a second home in the countryside. Few people own property abroad.

Rental prices tend to be highest in Tallinn's Old Town. It is easier to find property and lower rents in the Kesklinn ("town center"), and in the surrounding neighborhoods. The rental system is straightforward, as are rules relating to noise: you are expected not to disturb others between the hours of 11:00 p.m. and 7:00 a.m. You should respect the rules in your complex or neighborhood.

THE DAILY ROUND

On average, people live within thirty minutes' travel
from their work. Commuting between cities is quite
rare. The working day for those in public service
and in most offices begins at 8:30 or 9:00 a.m. and
lasts eight hours, although, in reality, many people
put in more hours than this. Longer days are,
inevitably, even more common in the private sector.
This is why a good working atmosphere and
good relationships with colleagues are
important, although not always
achievable. Estonians are not natural
team players, and tend to be
individualistic in their attitude to
work, especially in the business
sector. Many employees spend their
lunch break alone. Similarly, most
people would rather rush home after work than
join colleagues for a drink, especially if they have
families. Socializing at or through work is more
common among younger people. One uniting
tradition that has survived from the Soviet
occupation is the enthusiastic celebration of
birthdays in offices.

The school day generally begins at 8:00 a.m., and
after-school clubs and activities are offered for
children whose parents cannot pick them up at the
end of the school day (which can be as early as
1:00 p.m., though again this varies substantially).
On Fridays after work, many families head to
super/hypermarkets (such as Selver) on the

outskirts of cities to do their weekly shopping. Self-scanning is popular. A numbered ticket system usually operates at specialist counters in the larger supermarkets. There is an extra charge for plastic bags, and for this reason friends will often give you back a plastic bag in which you have brought them a present. There are few specialist delicatessens and boutiques, with the best, inevitably, being in Tallinn, selling handmade chocolate, French quiches, pastries, or fine wines. On weekends, if not during the week, most people spend time catching up with family. In summer, many city dwellers spend weekends in the countryside and take an extended break out of town to compensate for the long, dark winter.

PETS

Increasingly, owning a pedigree pet is something to aspire to. Dogs, in particular, are popular pets, and this is reflected in the popularity of magazines about pets and the number of pet shops. Dogs are not, however, normally welcome in restaurants, especially in towns and cities. Clinics and veterinarians issue pet passports in accordance with EU requirements.

chapter six

TIME OUT

You could be forgiven for thinking that the hardworking Lutheran Estonians have no time for leisure but, of course, they do. Going for a walk in the nearest forest or countryside is one of the most popular ways of winding down. In summer, there is a general exodus to the countryside. At all times of the year, swimming, visiting spas, and taking saunas are popular activities.

Despite the growing number of restaurants, most Estonians dine at home or with friends. Meeting in bars and cafés is becoming increasingly common, especially among younger people. As a visitor or tourist you are most likely to meet Estonians in bars and cafés, or at cultural events, and are unlikely to be invited to visit someone's home until a deeper bond of friendship has been formed.

Attendance at cultural events is generally high, so booking in advance is advisable. Concerts, in particular, are well attended and Estonians appear happy to pay for tickets that are, by local standards, relatively expensive.

IN THE COUNTRYSIDE

Estonians are rightly proud of the vast expanses of nature at their disposal, and make full use of them, whatever the weather or temperature. Solitary activities tend to be more popular than communal ones. Hiking, swimming, and, increasingly, cycling are favorite forms of exercise. Nordic walking, with ski poles, is a trend that has arrived from Scandinavia. Riding, sailing, and fishing are also popular. In summer, Estonians think nothing of

skinny-dipping in the country's many small lakes. Winter pastimes include cross-country skiing (the international Tartu marathon in February is Estonia's number one cross-country event), sledding, and skating. Rural sleigh rides on peasant-style sleds are great fun for adults and children alike. Extreme-sports fanatics can try kitesurfing on water or, in winter, ice. Good places for hiking include the Lahemaa, Matsalu, and Sooma nature reserves, and the islands.

SPORTS

Estonians are passionate about their sporting heroes, and consequently about the sports they excel in. When the wrestler Kristjan Palusalu won the country's first gold medal in 1936, the state awarded him a farm. Another well-remembered figure is the chess champion Paul Keres, who won eleven Olympic gold medals (1940–88) for the then Soviet Union. Tallinn was used for the yachting events at the 1980 Moscow Olympics; the Pirita TOP Spa and the Hotel Olümpia are perhaps the most visible reminders. In 1996, decathlete Erki Nool was elected "most popular Estonian," which may have spurred him on to claim gold at the Sydney Olympics in 2000; and when Kristina Smigun and Andrus Veerpalu between them scooped three gold medals for Estonia in the Turin Winter Olympics in 2006, the nation went wild with joy. Given the Estonian tendency to be loners, it is hardly surprising that all three were for individual cross-country skiing, rather than relay racing. The cyclist Jaan Kirsipuu won four Tour de France stages between 1999 and 2004. Estonia also has a good track record in ice-boat sailing, wrestling, and javelin-throwing.

Basketball is the most popular spectator sport. Interest in soccer is growing, though Estonia's soccer teams have failed to light up either the world stage or the European club scene. There are eight golf courses in the country, and Tallinn has several gyms, swimming pools, and tennis courts.

THE ARTS

Tallinn has the most vibrant cultural scene in
Estonia, although Tartu was the birthplace of
professional Estonian theater, the main artistic
movements, and alternative-rock festivals. Pärnu
has a strong theatrical culture and an impressive
new concert hall. Locals throughout the land are
keen event goers and, frustratingly for visitors,
most concerts and shows sell out fast, with
audiences healthily diverse in terms of both age
and class. For opera, ballet, or concerts by the
Philharmonic Chamber Choir, or featuring top
Estonian artists, it is essential to reserve weeks,
even months in advance. International pop artists
perform at the open-air Song Grounds stage.

The Estonian state actively promotes the arts.
One of the most expensive ventures in recent
years is the prestigious art museum Kumu, in
Kadriorg. The Estonian Opera and Concert Hall
(1905) and the Jugendstil Drama Theater have
both been renovated. The lemon-
and-cream opera house, funded by
local subscriptions before Estonia
established its independence, is
regarded with particular affection.
Renovation of the Russian-

language theater and the vast Russian cultural
center on Tallinn's Mere puiestee, once a cinema,
shows the state's commitment to funding Russian-
language as well as Estonian culture.

There is no central reservation service; you buy
tickets online, or at the venue's box office.

Cinema

Tallinn has three cinemas: the Coca-Cola Plaza, Kosmos, and Sōprus. Most large towns have just one, rather modest, cinema. For mainstream foreign movies, which are inevitably popular, it is wise to book in advance. Given the small size of the Estonian film industry, Estonian productions usually need foreign backing. Occasionally, a locally produced movie will make headlines abroad: Kristian Taska's *Names in Marble* (2002), about the fate of schoolboys who fought in Estonia's Independence War, won international acclaim, though more for its subject matter than its craft, and the "nostalgic" *Revolution of the Pigs* (2004), about Soviet summer camps, scooped the Jury Special Prize in Moscow. In terms of investment, the biggest recent production is *Lotte from the Inventors' Village*. Priit Pärn is Estonia's best-known director of animated movies, a genre in which Estonians excel. His depiction of totalitarianism in *Lunch on the Grass* (1987) remains a classic.

Movies are shown in the original language, with subtitles in Estonian and usually Russian, too. International sign/picture language is used to indicate a movie suitable for children.

Theater

Major theatrical productions are staged in Estonian or Russian, although nonnative speakers can usually enjoy musicals. The Estonian Drama

Theater (Eesti Draamateater) hosts mainly international and Estonian classics. Russian and Western European classics are the mainstay of the Russian Drama Theater (Veneteater). The other major Estonian-language theater in Tallinn is the Linnateater, which occupies several medieval houses in the Old Town, and holds open-air shows in its courtyard. Tallinn's Puppet Theater (Nukuteater) hosts shows for young people and children. The city's most experimental venue is Von Krahl.

Tartu's most prestigious venue is the Vanemuine Theater, which dates back to the 1860s, but was destroyed during the Second World War and rebuilt during the 1960s and 1970s. Some events are held in the older German Theater. Experimental theater is shown at the city's Harbor Theater (Sadamatheater). Pärnu's Endla Theater is the city's main venue for a variety of cultural happenings. Narva has a Russian-speaking theater group, Ilmarine, which cooperates with Tallinn's Russian Drama Theater. One of its goals is to introduce Estonian culture to Narva's Russian-speakers.

Music, Opera, and Dance
Every kind of live music is available in Estonia, and there is always something to see, whether lively rock bands in basement bars or world-class opera soloists. Tallinn's National Opera is the chief

opera and ballet venue. One of the country's most sought-after orchestras is the Estonian Philharmonic. Tartu's prestigious opera house, the Vanemuine, is named after the Estonian god of music. The opera and ballet seasons run from September to mid-June.

Estonia's greatest claim to international cultural fame is, unquestionably, through its music. This is thanks to the quality and originality of its choirs, conductors, and composers, among them Eri Klas, Neeme Järvi, his son, Paavo Järvi, and Ana Tali. Arvo Pärt, Erki Sven-Tüür, and Veljo Tormis, who specializes in modern renditions of ancient Finno-Ugric song, are the country's best-known composers. Singing, in particular, is a national strength. The world-renowned Estonian Philharmonic Chamber Choir, founded by Tõnu Kaljuste, who handed the baton to the UK's Paul Hillier, is the country's most prestigious choir. It is also well worth attending performances by the Boys' Choir, Men's Choir, or Ellerhein Girls' Choir. There is great enthusiasm for classical music, ranging from early and medieval music, energetically performed by Andres Mustonen's Hortus Musicus ensemble, to light operetta or challenging contemporary creations. Look out for the NYYD festival of contemporary music, which takes place in Tallinn in late October and early November.

In summer, Tallinn's Town Hall Square becomes the backdrop for free classical, rock, jazz, and folk concerts. Every year, Viljandi hosts an international folk festival. Every three years in July, Estonia hosts the Baltica Festival, an international folklore event that rotates between the three Baltic States. Its aim is to "preserve, revive, and develop national and regional cultural traditions." Tartu hosts the country's best rock festival, Plink Plonk. This is an open-air event, which festival organizers describe as "Roskilde with less dirt, Woodstock with less hassle." Most guests are from neighboring Scandinavia and the Baltic States. In autumn, Tartu hosts "Eclectica," an annual avant-garde festival favoring crossover between the arts.

Husband-and-wife team Agnes Oaks and Thomas Edur, mainstays of the English National Ballet, have helped to boost Estonia's reputation for producing talented classical ballet dancers. Names to look out for at Tallinn's National Opera include Marina Chirkova and Vladimir Arhangelski. There is also much local enthusiasm for contemporary dance, best seen at Tallinn's annual August Dance Festival. The event, led by the dancer and choreographer Mart Kangro, is a bold showcase for work by young choreographers.

Museums and Galleries
There are more than a hundred museums in Estonia, many of which have emerged since

the Soviet era—spectacularly so in the case of the Estonian Art Museum, Kumu, in Kadriorg, which opened in February 2006. The largest space of its kind in Scandinavia, this purpose-built venue houses works by leading Estonian artists from the nineteenth century to the present day, as well as temporary exhibitions on international trends.

Since the early 1990s, museum culture has been transformed. New takes on modern history feature at the Museum of Occupations, in Tallinn, and the chilling old KGB cells in Tartu. Fusty venues have been modernized, with admission fees consequently rising, though they remain inexpensive in many of the yet-to-be revamped venues. There are some spectacular spaces, too, from the Foreign Art Museum, in Peter the Great's Baroque palace in Kadriorg, to the Museum of Estonian Architecture, in a gorgeously converted limestone warehouse near the harbor. Dedicated museum hoppers should pick up the Tallinn Card from the tourist office, which offers free admission and unlimited public transportation. Attendance figures dropped after the restoration of independence, but with a higher, more stable standard of living in place, and more leisure time, numbers are on the rise.

There is still much to be done in terms of modernizing the smaller museums, some of which have an almost 1950s atmosphere and offer commentary only in Estonian. At best they can be quaintly charming, at worst clumsy and didactic.

FOOD AND DRINK
Eating Out
Although Tallinn has no shortage of smart eateries, dining out is still a rather formal event for most locals, and tends to be reserved for business meetings and special occasions; restaurants are still predominantly the realm of tourists, expats, and the better-off. Establishments in other towns, such as Tartu and Pärnu, tend to be more down-to-earth and less expensive. Since Estonians regained the ability to travel freely, they have brought back new ideas about dining and are more willing to experiment. Food from around the world, from Georgia and Korea to India and Italy, is all the rage, as are themed restaurants inspired by anything from apples or cheese to Tsarist Russia. Sometimes, the emphasis is on the presentation rather than fine food.

Neither Estonians nor Russian-speakers are natural vegetarians. There is only one vegetarian restaurant in Tallinn, although vegetarian dishes are increasingly available. Portions in mid-range eateries tend to be on the large side, and often one course will do. Estonian meat—pork and beef, rather than lamb, which is usually imported—and dairy products, especially yogurts, are particularly tasty. Local and seasonal specialties include sorrel, dill, summer berries, mushrooms, pike-perch, eel, herring with sour cream, sprats, elk, wild boar,

 *kodujuust* (cottage cheese), and *kama* (a mildly roasted mix of barley, grains, and pulses). Traditional country dishes include blood sausage, brawn, barley dishes, and pea soup. Bread, particularly dark rye bread (*leib*), is widely eaten and usually of good quality. German and Russian influences have made sauerkraut, borscht, and *seljanka* (a meaty soup) popular too. There are many regional cheeses, usually hard and not particularly flavorful. Ham and sausages tend to be strongly smoked. *Mulgi kapsas* (sauerkraut with bacon) is a specialty of Viljandi.

Traditionally, the main meal of the day is lunch, served in mid- or late afternoon, but this doesn't fit into office hours, so nowadays the main meal is generally eaten in the early evening.

It is wise to book in advance, especially for

dinner in a fashionable venue and during the
summer season, when restaurants may be
overwhelmed with cruise-ship tourists. Most
restaurants are open from noon until midnight;
dinner is generally served from 6:30 to 9:30 p.m.
Brasseries have not really caught on, but the few
that exist, such as Vertigo, offer excellent value. Most
cafés open at 9:00 or 10:00 a.m. Some bars close
only when the last customer leaves. It is always
possible to find something open, or a place to eat, in
the Old Town until 10:00 p.m. In fine weather,
many cafés have outside tables, especially those on
Town Hall Square, where it is worth paying more
for the scenic backdrop. Most cafés serve cakes and
savory snacks. Not all serve alcohol. In summer,
stalls in the Old Town sell Hanseatic-style sugared
almonds with cinnamon.

Drinks
Estonians are great coffee drinkers.
Some say this has to do with the
long, dark winters and the need
for a "kick" to keep going. Coffee
tends be strong, and most
establishments offer cappuccino, latte,
and espresso, as well as coffee served black, or
with cream.

The restoration of independence in 1991, and a
consequent increase in travel, brought new habits,
such as a fondness for wine rather than the
traditional vodka and beer. Popular local beers are
Saku, of which there are several varieties, and A le

Coq, a revived prewar lager from Tartu. Vodkas are also popular, with local blends including Viru Valge; Russian, Finnish, and Swedish brands are widely available. The island of Saaremaa produces a fresh-tasting gin. The dark, sticky, sweet *Vana Tallinn* liqueur is a popular souvenir gift, but is not to everyone's taste; many locals dismiss it as palatable only when served with ice cream. *Kristelküümu*, a caraway-seed liqueur, popular during the prewar Republic and now revived, is also an acquired taste, but one more favored by locals. Fruit-based country wines, including a pear-flavored sparkling wine, are produced in Põltsamaa, in the south. Several restaurants serve sweet Georgian red wines; Must Lammas, on Sauna, in Tallinn's Old Town, has a good range. Most top restaurants have international wine lists, at almost international prices.

Restaurant Etiquette
Staff in most restaurants are highly professional, if somewhat stiff. The service culture is still developing, so service with a smile is uncommon. There is an annoying tendency to remove finished plates when others at the table are still eating. Estonians tend not to linger long over a meal, unless the drink is flowing. Children are generally welcome in cafés and restaurants until 9:00 pm. Dogs are generally not welcome. Increasingly, restaurants have nonsmoking areas; the same cannot be said for cafés and bars. In most bars, the waiter brings your drinks to your table and

you pay for everything when you leave. Self-service is more common in pub-style bars, such as "Irish" establishments.

TIPPING

In some restaurants, a service charge is included in the bill. If not, tip 10 percent if you are happy with the service. You are not expected to tip in cafés or bars.

At beauty salons and hairdressers, customers usually tip 10 percent, but don't give more than EEK100.

It is customary to round up taxi fares.

SHOPPING

Though light-years away from the lines and shortages of the Soviet era, the Estonian retail experience is not the stuff of shopaholic dreams. When it comes to designer clothes, for example, there is little on offer that cannot be bought in other Western cities at roughly the same price. You can, however, find good-quality local products and produce (see below).

Tallinn is by far the best place to shop, with most of the interesting shops in the Vana Linn and Kesklinn. In the latter is the city's biggest shopping mall, Viru Keskus, which incorporates the former Soviet department store Kaubamaja. Architects have criticized the mall's bland design, of the kind you find in most Western cities, but

Tallinn needed something along these lines, and it is nothing if not convenient. Stockmann, a Finnish concern, is theoretically more upscale and pricier, but it only really beats Kaubamaja with its food hall. The passenger ferry and hydrofoil harbors are home to another concentration of shops, many of which sell souvenirs and alcohol, catering to tourists and day-trippers from Helsinki. Further out of Tallinn, toward the suburbs of Nõmme and Haabersti, hypermarkets stay open until 10:00 pm. The newest shopping complex is Ülemiste, by the airport.

Major credit cards are widely accepted in restaurants and shops. Most shops now use chip and PIN technology. ID is required for card transactions of more than EEK500.

Things Estonian

There are several Estonian craft shops in Tallinn's Old Town. Look out for the *kasitöö* sign, which guarantees that the goods stocked are authentic. Traditional items include linen, woven textiles and rugs, wrought ironwork, such as candlesticks, pokers, and so on, and chopping boards, butter knives, and serving spoons made out of fragrant juniper wood. Estonia has a strong tradition of natural health products, which is partly a hangover from Soviet days, when medicines were hard to come by; looking further back, Tallinn has one of the world's oldest apothecary stalls, on Town Hall Square, in business since the sixteenth century.

Look out for sea-buckthorn juice and blueberry juice, both "superfoods." Pharmacies sell sea-buckthorn oil for easing skin injuries and burns. You can also snap up delicious farm honey and flower-flavored syrups.

The Kalev chocolate factory produces fine, strong chocolate. See the "Drinks" section above (page 117) for further gift ideas. For children, you can find wooden toys, ceramic models of Tallinn's medieval dwellings, and attractive dolls' house furniture. If you under-estimated the winter chill, there's an abundance of knitwear based on traditional, often geometric, patterns. If you are a fan of Soviet memorabilia, it might be worth rifling through  secondhand and antiques shops, or visiting the Balti Jamm and Keskturg markets.

Finally, check out Tallinn's art galleries, where you can buy works by established local artists. Recommended addresses include Draakoni Galerii (Pikk 18), Haus (Uus 17), Vaal (Tartu maantee 80), Kaks (for glassware; on Lühike jalg), and A-Galerii (for handmade jewelry; Hobusepea 2). Don't miss Nu Nordik (Vabaduse väljak 8), which stocks trendy, affordable creations, such as glassware, ceramics, clothes, and handbags by young Estonian designers.

Store Hours

Store hours in the cities are usually 9:30 or 10:00 a.m. to 6:00 or 7:00 p.m., from Monday to Saturday. Shopping malls and hypermarkets often stay open longer in the evenings, to 8:00 or 9:00 p.m.; some are open on Sundays. Few shops close for lunch. In smaller towns you may find local convenience stores that stay open late and are open on Sunday; but don't bank on this if your lodging doesn't include meals.

Markets

The best markets are in the capital. The Keskturg, near the international bus station, is best for fresh and pickled produce, including chanterelle mushrooms (*kukkusenned*), seasonal berries, fresh sorrel, and gherkins. Near the railway station, the Balti Jaam (railway) market has all kinds of junk and a bustling atmosphere. Craft markets are frequently held in Tallinn's Town Hall Square, especially during the summer months, Old Town Days, and at Christmas, when craftwork and festive specialties can be found in the vaulted basement of the Town Hall.

Banking

Banking hours are generally Monday to Friday, 9:00 a.m. to 5:00 p.m. Some Hansapank branches are open until 6:00 p.m. Many banks are open on Saturdays from 9:00 a.m. to 3:00 p.m. They do not close for lunch, but are closed on state holidays.

Seventy percent of Estonians bank online. Outside banking hours, foreign-exchange kiosks (in the larger shopping centers and bus and railway stations), big hotels, and travel agents will change money. Modern Estonia is a card- rather than cash-oriented society (though you won't be asked for identity when paying in cash). Checks and traveler's checks are not used. There is no shortage of ATMs in Tallinn and other big towns; these accept Visa, Eurocard, Mastercard, and Maestro/Cirrus, but not usually American Express.

chapter seven

TRAVELING

Public transportation in Estonia is inexpensive compared with prices in countries such as the UK. The privatized and inefficient railway system is now back in state hands, and everyone hopes that the service will improve. The most popular

form of long-distance transportation within the country is the bus; the network is efficient and offers good value for the money. Locals tend to be quiet (except when on their cell phones) and private when traveling. You would not expect to strike up a conversation with strangers, or share food with them. That

said, any attempt on your part to converse is unlikely to be rebuffed. More and more people now own cars, and prefer to travel around the country in their own vehicles, although the quality of the roads is sometimes poor. The better-off may well see traveling by public transportation as something that is beneath them.

TRAINS

Unless you're hell-bent on reducing your carbon footprint, or planning a trip to Russia, the Estonian rail network is unlikely to be your preferred method of getting from city to city. Within Estonia, buses are more frequent, cheaper, and more reliable, the result of underinvestment in the rail network and the decision to follow the UK route and privatize the network, rather than opt for a state-run continental model; as any disgruntled British commuter will tell you, this was a disastrous idea, with profit taking primacy over customer service. The network has now been renationalized, but it will take a while for any benefits to filter through.

There are three main train companies in Estonia: GoRail, which runs services from Tallinn to Moscow, via Narva; Edelaraudtee, which covers the main domestic destinations from the capital, including Tartu, Pärnu, Narva, and Viljandi; and Elektrikiraudtee, which serves Tallinn's suburbs and neighboring towns, and is thus perhaps the most useful for the visitor. The main station in Tallinn is the Balti Jaam. Once notorious for drug dealing and muggings, it has had cash pumped into it in recent years and been transformed, with a hotel, a day spa, and a designer café among the improvements. You can buy tickets for the Moscow service at the ticket offices in the main hall; for domestic services, buy a ticket on the train or at a touch-screen vending machine.

BUSES, STREETCARS, AND TROLLEY BUSES

The best way of getting around within Estonia, and of visiting the other Baltic States, is by bus. Ecolines (www.ecolines.net) runs direct services from Tallinn to Riga and Vilnius, via Pärnu, and to Kiev, via Tartu. The Web site offers information on times and fares in English; you can buy tickets online or at Tallinn's bus station (Bussiterminal). Domestic services are run by Bussi Reisid (www.bussireisid.ee), which has direct and stopping services to Tartu, Pärnu, Narva, Viljandi, Rakvere, Haapsalu, and Saaremaa.

Within Tallinn, the public-transportation network comprises a mix of buses, trams, and trolleybuses; there is no metro system, and there is no public transport within the compact Old Town. The main transport hubs are the Viru Keskus shopping center, the Balti Jaam, and Vabaduse väljak, on the southern edge of the Old

Town. Regular services run between 6:00 a.m. and 11:00 p.m., with reduced schedules on Saturdays and Sundays. Pick up route maps at the Tallinn Tourist Office, at the bus station, or at the underground terminus in Viru Keskus.

Make sure that you have a valid ticket before getting on public transportation, or buy one from the driver immediately on entering. If you need to buy a ticket, enter at the front; tickets are sold only at stops, not while the vehicle is moving. Bus, trolley, and tram tickets can be purchased at newsstands for 10 EEK or from the driver for 15 EEK. You can also by a 10-ticket package for 85 EEK or a day pass for 45 EEK. The Tallinn Card (www.tourism.tallinn.ee) offers free travel on public transportation. Punch your ticket right after entering at one of the machines on the bus, trolley, or tram. Passengers traveling with fake tickets or without tickets will be fined.

There is a bus network in Tartu; in other towns, you should be able to get around on foot.

TAXIS

Taxis are inexpensive by Western European standards, but prices have risen as the economy has blossomed, as, unfortunately, have instances of sharp practice or opportunism by rogue drivers. Individual companies are allowed to set their own tariffs, which can make it harder to know if you're being ripped off. However, there are a few measures you can take to protect yourself. Check that the meter is turned on, and that there is a price list clearly displayed on the dashboard and/or a window in the back. This should indicate the metered rate of fare; the per-kilometer charge, with night rates applicable from 11:00 p.m. until 6:00 a.m.; and a waiting charge. If in doubt, ask for a price in advance, though bear in mind that not all drivers speak English; as a rule of thumb, a journey from the airport to the Old Town should cost less than 150 EEK. And ask for a receipt from the meter's printer; if this isn't provided, you can refuse to pay the fare.

On the plus side, there is no charge for booking a taxi by telephone, and you'll rarely wait more than ten minutes for one. Taxi stands are located at major intersections and in front of bigger hotels; you can choose from any of the available taxis at a taxi stand, or hail one on the street. Note that there is limited access for cars in the Old Town, which can add ten to fifteen minutes to journey times.

BICYCLE TAXIS

Velotaxis are a fun, environmentally friendly way to get around the center of Tallinn. These sturdy rickshaw taxis powered by young people operate from March to October. For more information, visit www.velotakso.ee.

BOATS

Tallinn's heritage as a maritime city lives on in its extensive connections to Scandinavia, primarily to Finland and Sweden. Several firms offer car and passenger ferry services to Helsinki and Stockholm (overnight), departing from the main passenger port, the Reisisadam (www.portoftallinn.com); in summer, there are also fast catamarans between Tallinn and Helsinki, as well as passenger hydrofoils, which arrive at the Linnahall (www.lindaliini.ee).

Ferries, albeit of a humbler nature, are also the prime routes from the mainland to the islands. Services to Saaremaa, the biggest island, depart from Virtsu, near Haapsalu (www.slk.saaremaa.ee).

DRIVING

The arrival of Western cars in a country long accustomed to the Russian Lada has been something of a mixed blessing. Estonians have been almost too keen to exercise their newfound choice, with a powerful car something of a status symbol, especially among young men, and after independence, this led to a high death rate and a good deal of aggression on the roads. Things have calmed down in recent years, but foolhardy passing maneuvers remain too frequent—if in doubt, pull over sharply—and drivers do not always keep a safe distance from the vehicle in front of them. In addition, they do not always signal when turning, and often use their hazard lights to say "thank you." Use of the horn is almost unheard of.

The roads, too, leave much to be desired, in terms both of the surface and of their size: even the "freeways" have only one lane in each direction, which can make driving wearing. Speed limits reflect this: 31 mph (50 kmph) in towns, 55 mph (90 kmph) out of town, and 68 mph (110 kmph) on the fastest roads. You're unlikely to run out of gas, however, as stations are plentiful, at least on major roads. There is zero tolerance for drunk driving, and headlights must be kept on at all times, with snow tires compulsory in winter. In rural areas, you should heed signs warning of elk crossing. In Tallinn, trams and trolleybuses have priority over cars, and there is limited access for cars in the heavily pedestrianized Old Town. On-street parking in city centers must be paid for, but in a typically Estonian show of pragmatism, there's a fifteen-minute grace period (leave a note on the windshield or dashboard to show the time you parked. In some cases, parking restrictions apply only in the daytime and/or on weekdays; in Tallinn's Old Town, however, parking fees are a twenty-four-hour affair.

In the event of an accident, emergency numbers are 110 for the police and 112 for an ambulance. Many foreign driver's licenses are accepted, including, of course, the EU driver's license, but US citizens will need an international driver's license. Anyone driving their own car into Estonia must carry the original vehicle registration documents. The Estonian Border Guard will impound your vehicle if you don't. Those planning to visit Russia should also take an International Certificate for Motor Vehicles. You will also need a Green Card confirming that you have adequate coverage. A hazard-warning triangle must be carried and displayed in the event of a breakdown. The Automobile Club of Estonia (Eesti Autoklubi) offers an emergency service; nonmembers will pay a premium for assistance. The number to call for roadside vehicle assistance and towing service is 1888.

To rent a car, you must be over twenty-one and have possessed a driver's license for at least two years. Local rental agencies tend to be cheaper than the international chains.

CYCLING

Being largely flat and at worst gently hilly, Estonia is an ideal place for a spot of two-wheeled exploration, particularly in the unspoiled and largely car-free rural areas. Beyond the cobbled Old Town, Tallinn has a developing network of cycle lanes; the ride out to Pirita, with views across the sea to the city spires, is spectacular. Bicycle rental is available in most towns, and vacation centers or tourist farms will have bikes to hire or borrow: even on the remotest islands, you're likely to encounter a group of Estonian cyclists in full gear, on a corporate outing or reunion weekend. There are several marked routes covering the whole country, mostly avoiding main roads; for details, visit www.bicycle.ee.

WALKING

There are pedestrianized areas in most Estonian cities: the Old Town in Tallinn is probably the most notable example, and it can be something of a shock to emerge into the hustle, bustle, and traffic of the modern center. The cobblestones and uneven sidewalks can be difficult to negotiate, particularly with a child's stroller, and winter walking can be perilous (though local women traverse the icy cobbles on four-inch stiletto heels!). Watch out, too, for falling icicles. Many locals have adopted the Scandinavian practice of Nordic walking, in which ski poles are used, even in the absence of snow.

Beyond the cities, Estonia is a walker's paradise, with endless forests and organized trails on the islands and in protected areas such as the national park of Lahemaa. The low population density means you'll hardly see a soul as you ramble.

WHERE TO STAY

It's less than two decades since your only accommodation choice in Tallinn was between the three Intourist hotels, the hulking Viru, and the newer but equally hulking Olümpia, built for the Olympics in 1980, and the dingy Hotel Tallinn. All three are still there today, but they have been transformed: as has Tallinn's hotel scene, which offers a typically Western range of expensive luxury and cheap simplicity and caters to businessmen and boutiquistas alike. Some offer reduced rates for long stays, and there is a growing apartment rental market, offering weekly or monthly rents, including some stunning properties within the Old Town walls. Business hotels drop rates on weekends, and prices drop dramatically in winter, the dead season as far as tourism is concerned, except for New Year.

Inevitably, the capital has seen the biggest boom in hotel building, so there is less diversity beyond it, but Tartu and Pärnu both have options for any budget. There are also some excellent options in the countryside and on the islands, and some of the many tourist farms have geared themselves toward the corporate team-building market.

You can find detailed accommodation listings on the Web sites of the Tallinn City Tourism Office and Convention Bureau (www.tourism.tallinn.ee) and Visit Estonia (www.visitestonia.com), though neither offers a reservation service; contact the hotel direct or use a local tourism agency. Booking well in advance is essential in summer and recommended throughout the year. Quoted prices should be per room, including breakfast and tax.

Hotels are graded from one to five stars according to a strictly defined series of criteria set out by the Ministry of Economic Affairs. However, these relate to facilities rather than location, charm, or cost. A hotel with fewer than ten rooms is categorized as a guesthouse, and must offer food on site; hostels do not provide meals but have cooking facilities. Some Estonian hostels are registered with HI (Hostelling International); the Estonian Youth Hostels Association (www.hostels.ee) is a member of the International Youth Hostel Federation, and its Web site offers a booking service. There are dozens of campsites in Estonia, many of which also offer simple cottage accommodation; they are often attached to tourist farms, spas, or holiday centers, making them ideal bases for exploring the countryside. For more details, visit www.turismiweb.ee.

HEALTH

Visitors from abroad must have valid health insurance for the duration of their stay; this can be purchased at the border. EU citizens are covered, but should bring their European Health Insurance Cards.

The cost of private health and dental care is still lower than in many Western countries, hence the steady flow of "health tourists," particularly from Scandinavia.

Pharmacies—called "Apteek" and recognizable by the universal green cross—are well stocked, and plentiful; pharmacists tend to have a high level of expertise. In summer, especially if you will be visiting coastal areas, it is best to take mosquito repellent.

SAFETY AND SECURITY

Estonia is a generally a safe country in which to travel. Tallinn once had a reputation as a center for organized crime, but today the crime rate is low, and the main risk to a traveler is probably a road accident, although pickpockets are not uncommon in Tallinn's Old Town and at stations. You should also be careful when entering and leaving bars and nightclubs, although this is really only common sense.

There have also been reports of credit-card fraud and Internet-based crime, including financial scams. Car theft, which soared in the 1990s, has dwindled, but still occurs. Violent crimes are rare. Generally, Estonians say they feel safe in Estonia, but concede that they keep an eye on their possessions—again, only common sense.

Tallinn has a rising rate of heroin addiction, and the authorities have a zero-tolerance approach to drug possession, with prison sentences of up to ten years.

Identity Documents

Identity cards are now mandatory for Estonians aged fifteen or over, and for permanent foreign residents. Typically, in this technology-mad country, they can be used for a variety of purposes, including a digital signature for Internet transactions and e-voting. The government envisages adding work security passes, bank cards, and health details to the one card. Visitors should carry a passport at all times.

If you intend to stay in Estonia for longer than three months, you will need to obtain a residence permit from the Estonian Citizenship and Migration Board (www.mig.ee/eng). There are strict quotas on immigration, but ethnic Estonians and citizens of the EU, the USA, Norway, Iceland, Switzerland, and Japan are exempt from these. The Web site above has detailed information about applying for temporary or permanent residence; or contact the Estonian embassy in your country.

The Police

Driving is the activity most likely to bring you into contact with the Estonian police. Estonians, who have a general mistrust of authority, have little regard for the police, with traffic cops particularly disliked: Estonian motorists will flash their headlights at oncoming traffic to indicate a police presence on the road ahead. Police officers often speak little or no English. If you are unlucky enough to be robbed or burgled, you will need to report the crime at the nearest police station, where you will receive the documentation necessary for an insurance claim.

chapter eight

BUSINESS BRIEFING

Estonia's economy has developed with dramatic speed since the restoration of independence in 1991, making nonsense of the Soviet Union's claim that Estonians would be plunged into poverty without Big Brother. Boosted by liberal taxation policies, a relatively inexpensive but skilled and well-educated workforce, modern telecommunications systems, and the country's perfect position for east-west transit trade, the economy has grown at an average of nearly 6 percent since 1995. Current predictions point to continued annual growth between 5 and 6 percent. Successive governments have gone out of their way to attract foreign investment, most notably via low taxation—there is a flat rate of 22 percent, and companies that reinvest profits in their business are exempt from corporate tax (also 22 percent). Some

observers, however, believe the latter policy may change before the end of the next decade, largely because of complaints of unfair competition from the EU, but there has also been talk of the government wanting to reduce corporate tax further. Estonia's currency, the kroon, originally pegged to the Deutschmark, has been pegged to the euro since 1999, at a rate of 15.65 kroons per euro.

Estonia's economic success story has seen it dubbed a "Baltic Tiger," and the country has established itself as one of the world's best places to do business. Among other indicators, it had the seventh-freest economy of 157 countries assessed in 2006 by the *Wall Street Journal* and the Heritage Foundation's Index of Economic Freedom; it was rated the twentieth-most competitive state out of 104, and hence most competitive of the EU new member states, by the World Economic Forum's Current Competitiveness Index (2005–6); and it came sixteenth out of 155 countries in the World Bank "Doing Business" report (2006). Estonia has also earned high international credit ratings, among them Moody's (A1), Standard & Poor's (A, outlook positive), and Fitch (A, outlook positive).

The Estonian economy is centered on medium and small businesses, rather than heavy industry. The most popular sectors for investment in recent years have been machinery and equipment such as computer hardware and software, transport and transit trade, and real estate (now more for locals, as the market for foreign investors is more or less saturated). The food-service industry is still developing, as is the sector on renewable energies. The government, for its part, has been investing in rural infrastructure.

Many of the most successful local businesses, including the pan-Baltic Hansapank bank, are now foreign-owned (principally by Scandinavian companies). Estonian Air is part-owned by SAS and the successful Estonian-founded Reval hotel group is now in Norwegian hands. Foreign investors, via Estonian companies they have taken over, are also using Estonia as a base for investing in Latvia and Lithuania.

FAMILY FIRMS AND MULTINATIONALS
Medium and small businesses in the domestic sector are thriving. The development of family enterprises, and of a growing middle class, is reflected in the fast-growing tourism sector and the rising number of restaurants, cafés, and boutique hotels. Family businesses also include the manufacture of chocolates, natural health and cosmetic products, and beauty salons. In the countryside, many families involved in agriculture have switched to tourism, hence the rise in the number of bed-and-breakfast establishments and tourist farms. A large part of the growth in tourism is related to cruise-ship day-trippers and centered on Tallinn's small Old Town, so successive Estonian governments have been keen

to encourage longer stays beyond the Old Town, in the countryside, and on the islands.

Multinationals are most attracted to the financial sector, where, despite the growing number of local managers, there are still a number of foreign (Western) managers in senior management.

GOVERNMENT AND BUSINESS

Successive governments have continued to promote foreign investment, enabling foreign businesses to compete on a level playing field with local ones: they have equal rights and obligations, and there are no special restrictions. VAT is 18 percent and social tax is 33 percent (20 percent social security, 13 percent medical insurance). The legal system follows the continental model and is influenced by Germany's. Estonia has a reputation for being transparent and relatively free of red tape, especially when compared to other former Communist countries, including Latvia and Lithuania. Foreign businesspeople still warn that, no matter how firm an agreement or deadline may appear, it is essential to check agreements thoroughly and highlight anything that is unclear before it becomes a problem—especially given the characteristic Estonian reticence and reluctance to openly question a situation.

Although Estonian politicians are often criticized for promoting the businesses interests of their friends and contacts, local politics has not deterred foreign investors, who usually say they are more than satisfied with the government's noninterventionist approach. It is generally easy to get things done. Enterprise Estonia, part of the Estonian Investment Agency, provides much useful advice on doing business in Estonia (www.investinestonia.com).

THE ESTONIAN WORKFORCE

Unions are weak and do not constitute an obstacle to doing business. Entry to the European Union has led to a labor shortage, particularly in the building and medical sectors. Employment is high and so is mobility. Earning well is a top priority and Estonians are generally prepared to put in long hours to achieve this goal, even if it means taking work home on weekends. Theoretically, the length of the working day is eight hours, and employees have twenty-eight days' vacation. Employment contracts should be terminated in writing, unless otherwise agreed upon by both parties. Unemployment benefit is low, and the much-touted "Lutheran work ethic" also means that not being employed is generally seen as shameful and "your own fault."

Local employees are generally reliable, proud, and hardworking, but tend to be poor communicators, reluctant to raise problems, and quick to take constructive criticism personally. They are not natural team players. Foreigners working in the rapidly developing service sector say that it is still difficult to find extroverted Estonians who can put on a cheerful facade, look relaxed, or approach sales with gusto. One foreign businessman with extensive experience in the country comments: "I do not understand how they stay alive this way. Even if you want to buy a new car, you have to pull the information out of the salesman." This may come across as "Soviet," but is more the result of reticence and a feeling that aggressive sales tactics are vulgar, undignified, and embarrassing.

WOMEN IN BUSINESS

Around 30 percent of businesspeople are women, and more and more women are creating their own businesses. There is also a growing number of Estonian women in senior positions, for example in banking, although they tend to earn less than their male counterparts. Foreign businesswomen are generally welcome in Estonia and it is perfectly acceptable for them to invite local male or female counterparts out to dinner. Similarly, foreign businessmen can offer to invite Estonian businesswomen out to eat, although this is not considered "necessary" for getting on with business.

Generous maternity and paternity policies are in place, but a lack of affordable child care places and inequality in salaries mean that it is women, rather than men, who usually take leave following the birth of a child.

DOING BUSINESS: A MINI-GUIDE

To understand an Estonian company's management culture, you need to spend time within it. There is a huge variety of companies in Estonia, many of them run and staffed by people who are much younger than their foreign counterparts, and who favor an informal, democratic, consultative approach.

In general, Estonians are less hierarchical than Russian-speakers. Local managers tend to be more forthright and authoritarian when dealing with locals and employees than with foreign workers and managers.

Estonia's business culture is not generally formal, and etiquette is by no means set in stone. Be sensitive, however, to the fact that some businesses may be predominantly either Estonian-speaking or Russian-speaking. Businesses are more likely to be the latter in Russian-speaking areas such as northeastern Estonia. However, cultural differences will vary hugely depending on the activity, rather than language of each company or business. As a crude generalization, Russian-speaking businesspeople may appear more extroverted and conversational, and may be more likely to socialize, although this is neither more nor less likely to lead to a business deal. It is also wise to remember that many people in the local business sector know each other, so be careful about criticizing others.

Making Contacts and Appointments

It is best not to show up without an appointment, not because it would be seen as impolite, but because people tend to be extremely busy, and you may not be able to meet anyone at such short notice. It is not necessary to write a letter, although you may feel more comfortable doing so in the first instance. It is perfectly usual to introduce yourself and send background material by e-mail. It is wise to reconfirm appointments a couple of days beforehand. A word of warning: a high percentage of business communication is conducted by e-mail, so compose your messages clearly and correctly, as if writing a letter. The content will be treated formally.

Watch the Time!

In Estonian the half hour is counted *before* the hour, not after it: half past eight can be expressed as "*pole ühekse*"—literally "half of nine." Estonians may therefore misunderstand a time you are conveying, so it is wise to say, for example, "8:30" rather than "half past eight," and to give a time according to the twenty-four-hour clock to be on the safe side. Most Estonians are punctual. If you are going to be even five minutes late, you would be expected to telephone or text in advance (all businesspeople have cell phones, and often leave them on during meetings). To arrive thirty minutes late, even with a convincing excuse, would not go down well.

Language

Most Estonian businesspeople speak English well, and you can safely assume that a meeting will be conducted in English. Any attempt to speak Estonian would be appreciated and might help to break the ice, although Estonians would inevitably respond in English unless you were fluent.

Some Russian-speakers, however, particularly those in middle management, don't speak English well, so if you don't speak Russian, you would do well to employ a translator. Although Estonian is the sole official language, producing marketing material in Russian would obviously help penetrate the Russian-speaking market in Estonia.

Dress Code

On the whole, Estonian men dress conservatively but not formally, preferring a smart-casual approach. Although they may be impressed by brand names, they are unlikely to judge you by your clothes. Wearing a tie is optional.

Women are more likely to dress formally or power-dress. The quality of your clothes is more likely to impress than the style. Ostentatious dressing is not the norm and may be unnerving.

Business Cards

Generally, people present business cards immediately, and expect you to do the same. It is perfectly acceptable for these to be in English, perhaps with a translation in the appropriate language on the back.

Meetings
Meetings generally last thirty minutes, and there is little small talk. They are not particularly formal. It is advisable to shake hands only at important, high-level meetings; even then, men are more likely to shake hands; don't offer your hand to a woman unless she offers hers. Let the "host side" set the tone. You may introduce yourself to all present by first name and surname, or even by first name only. Using surnames after a first meeting may come across as overly frosty. There is no need to draw up an agenda for a sales meeting or a less formal affair, only for a longer and more detailed meeting. Know your facts and figures, and present them clearly; Estonians are not impressed by spin. They are pragmatic and, above all, look for commonsense and practical ideas and solutions.

Despite this no-frills approach, presentations tend to be high-tech. It is not always easy to break the ice, but a well-timed wry joke will help. Estonians are proud, even prickly; any attempt to lecture or talk down to them will be quietly despised. During a first meeting, it is polite not to answer your mobile telephone, though Estonians tend to do this all the time. This may strike foreigners as rude, but is not intended so.

Negotiation and Decision Making
It is important for Estonians to build up trust, in particular with a view to promises being kept. Given that so many people know each other, it is

useful to build up connections and use contacts wherever possible. Negotiating usually involves a lot of listening and agreeing, but may be followed up by an e-mailed "no." You need patience.

There is no strong tradition of negotiating, so do not make an unreasonable offer in the hope that this will lead to haggling and settlement; instead, be realistic from the start. Estonians are not confrontational and may be reluctant to say "no" to your face. You may not know what they are thinking (what is unsaid often speaks volumes) until they send you a message, almost certainly by e-mail. They like to reflect and may strike foreigners as rather unfriendly. That said, agreement may be reached rapidly; there is no standard. Getting to the point and presenting the facts in a straightforward way can help to speed things up. Although locals are highly protective of their private lives, especially when they have a family, it is acceptable to telephone a business associate at home in the evening up until 9:00 p.m., even 10:00 p.m. if it is important. Remember, too, that Estonians are prone to understatement, so if someone says "*normalne*" ("that's normal"), they may well be indicating that something is "fine," even "great." If anything that resembles enthusiasm is shown, this is a good sign. A similar response from Russian-speakers may not indicate the same level of interest.

The final decision will usually be made by top management and, in this sense, local companies tend to be very hierarchical. One problem that foreign managers frequently contend with is a reluctance, or even an inability, on the part of both Estonian- and Russian-speaking employees to admit mistakes, either individually or collectively. There may also be a tendency to give customers the impression that any mistake made is theirs.

Business Dining

Entertainment is not an important or necessary part of doing business in Estonia. Deals are made in the office, and if you attend a business lunch it will be brief. You are more likely to be invited out to dinner once business has been settled.

Follow-up

It is essential to follow up all meetings as soon as possible, especially if the local party has shown any reticence. This is almost always done via e-mail; only invoices tend to be sent as letters. If you decide not to go ahead with a deal, you can communicate this via e-mail or letter. Contracts may also be drawn up and confirmed by e-mail. It is acceptable and advisable to send Christmas or New Year greetings cards to business colleagues as a way of staying in touch. If you have Russian-speaking employees or associates, remember that they celebrate Christmas and Easter two weeks later than Estonians and other Westerners do. Nobody would expect you to know this, but such a greeting or message would be much appreciated.

COMMUNICATING

Estonian is a Finno-Ugric language, a small group that includes Finnish (to which it is closely related), Hungarian, and Lappish. The first syllable is always stressed, vowels are strong and clear, and there's a pronounced rhythm. It is a phonetically straightforward but grammatically complex language, with no article, but fourteen cases. There are also no words for "he" or "she," only *tema*—"one" or "it."

WHICH LANGUAGE?

It puzzles and may indeed annoy Estonians that so many foreigners ask what language is spoken in Estonia. The answer is simple: Estonian is the official language and English is the most popular foreign language, spoken by people of all types and ethnic origin. So why the confusion? Well, Russian was the language of the Soviet occupiers, and 29.7 percent of Estonia's population are officially considered to be Russian-speaking, with by far the highest concentration in northeastern Estonia and Tallinn. The Russian-speaking community includes Belarusians, Ukrainians, and a large part of the local Jewish community. Today, approximately 40 percent of Tallinners speak Russian as their first language. Increasingly, English and Estonian are also spoken. Society is, however, still segregated, with people talking about "Estonian" or "Russian" cafés, clubs, kindergartens, and so on. There are few mixed partnerships or marriages. Many Russian-speakers live in largely Russian-speaking areas, such as Lasnamäe, rather than the more Estonian, pre-Soviet suburb of Nõmme or in the Old Town. Most of the Russian-language schools are in Tallinn and Ida Virumaa, in northeastern Estonia.

Strictly speaking, it is correct to refer to Russian-speakers as exactly that, but most Estonians simply say "Russians." The important point for the foreigner is to be sensitive to this linguistic divide: never assume that a local can or wants to speak Russian unless you are sure. You may occasionally come across an Estonian and a Russian-speaker communicating in each other's language, in order to practice it, or as a gesture of goodwill. Estonians born in or after the late 1980s have probably had little or no exposure to the Russian language, so if they are unable to speak it this is not necessarily a sign of reluctance. The best advice, if you speak Russian, is to ask politely whether you may use it before plunging in.

Many of those employed in the service sector are Russian-speakers. A recent study of the language skills of taxi drivers in Tallinn showed that many of them had insufficient knowledge of Estonian and did not speak good English either. Many people in northern Estonia, including Tallinn, who had illicit access to Finnish television during the Soviet era, speak Finnish, hence the number of both skilled and unskilled Estonians who seek work in Finland. This is becoming increasingly rare, however, for young people under the age of twenty. Locals who attended school during the Nazi occupation (1941–4) may know some German. English is widely understood, especially in Tallinn and Tartu, and by younger people generally. Older people in rural areas will not necessarily speak any English.

Inevitably, the language divide could also be seen as a cultural one. Foreign visitors are often surprised by the speed with which locals can identify who is Estonian or Russian, simply by their looks or by observing their manners. Although these two cultures have, of course, influenced each other to a degree, even imperceptibly, visitors are likely to be struck by a clear culture clash. In crude clichés, "Russians" are more likely to talk loudly, to invade your personal space, and to be generally more extroverted, even friendly and helpful; Estonians are more likely to be quiet and introverted, and may come across as frosty, especially at a first meeting. There are also differences in religion and rituals, such as the timing of celebrations and festivals—the Estonian Christmas is on December 25, the Russian Christmas on January 6.

Remember that any attempt to speak a few words of Estonian, even just to say thank you, will be gratefully received, although often with surprise. Unfortunately, if you are struggling with the language, most locals will switch to English, thus making it hard to practice. Finally, if you are a Russian-speaker and keen to tune into the Russian-language media, you are more likely to learn about what is going on in Estonia from the few Russian-language TV programs than from reports coming out of Russia about Estonia, which are often skewed. This may be reflected in the local Russian press as well, however.

WRITTEN COMMUNICATION

Written communication is much more formal than spoken conversation, whatever culture you are dealing with. Informal e-mail writing, however, is widespread, as the introduction of the Internet coincided with the rebuilding of the country following the restoration of independence in 1991. There is no single correct way in English to end the most formal of letters: "Yours sincerely" (*lugupidamisega*) or "Kind regards" (*tervitades*) are both perfectly acceptable. In general, it is best to keep language simple, plain, and direct; there is no need for florid forms of address. In e-mails, those who know each other well often sign off with *päikest!* (sunshine). Estonians are generally enthusiastic about new technology. They like the impersonality and freedom from small talk it provides, and many prefer to handle work issues by e-mail rather than telephone. Texting to friends on cell phones is very common.

FORMS OF ADDRESS

The standard abbreviated titles used in addressing letters in Estonian are: *Lp Proua* Thomson ("*Lugupeetud*," meaning "honored," and "*Proua*" meaning "Mrs."). "*Preili*" ("Miss") is considered old-fashioned, and it is much more common to use the abbreviation *Pr.* ("Ms"). There is also *v.a.*, "very honored." For a man you say *Härra*, or *Hr.*

There are different words for the singular and the plural, or polite, forms of "you," "*sina*" and "*teie*," respectively. The latter is much more formal. If in doubt, use the polite form, *teie*.

At work, colleagues may quickly start using *sina*, even if there is a significant gap in age or position. People of the same profession often use *sina* right away. *Teie* is initially used to address clients outside the office. In the past it was used much more, and the transition to *sina* took much longer. There is no single rule about when or where to use which form. It depends on age (younger people use *sina* much more than *teie*, including to people they have just met) and on the relationship. Those serving in banks, shops, and ticket offices use *teie*, as do customers, even regular customers, for example at the hairdresser. For older people, the transition is usually achieved by proposing a switch to *sina*. With others there may be no clear moment, and *sina* simply slips in. Interestingly, those trying to avoid the issue altogether may revert to peculiarly impersonal sentences, such as, "What does one think?" instead of "What do you think?" Bear in mind that it is possible in Estonian to address someone by his or her first name and *teie*, for example, Johann, *teie*. This is not an expression of lack of respect; nor is it intended as one when translated into English.

FACE-TO-FACE
Greetings and Conversations

Shaking hands is the most usual form of greeting when meeting someone new, and even an acquaintance, whether you are being introduced or saying hello or good-bye. Cheek kissing is rare, and might be considered rather pretentious. If you want to risk it, one peck is sufficient, but it is much more usual to greet good friends with a hug. Men usually shake hands. Slapping on the back is not common, and may be seen as patronizing, or as an invasion of personal space.

It is usual to look at other people in the street, even in Tallinn, if only because it's likely that you will see someone you know (certainly, that's how locals see it). People mutter "*Tere*" (hello) at any time of the day, sometimes only briefly, as an indication that they have spotted you. It is polite to acknowledge shop assistants or employees in the post office, restaurants, and cafés with "*Tere*," which is acceptable whatever the native language of the person you are addressing. You should do the same with a group of people, such as parents waiting to collect children from nursery or school. In all these situations, it is perfectly acceptable to say just "*Tere*," and not to indicate whether it is morning or afternoon. It is, however, also quite common to hear, "*Tere homikust*" (good morning) or "*Tere õhtust*" (good evening). Estonians who know each other well may also greet each other with "*Hommik*"—a bit like saying "Morning."

There is little intonation in Estonian, which is why Estonians speaking English may sound flat, or even come across as brusque and grumpy, when they are in fact being perfectly polite.

Reticence and Modesty

Estonians don't engage in much small talk. Plain, direct speech and saying what you mean are what is valued. To follow a greeting with "How are you?" may be seen as a personal question that requires an honest, in-depth answer, beginning with "I'm not at all well!" Mentioning the weather as part of a greeting is not usual either.

Estonians do not usually compliment one another unprompted, for example to say, "You are looking well today." Nor are they forthcoming with praise, and may also be rather awkward about receiving it, responding that they could have done better, or really have not achieved anything worthy of note.

Estonians are generally polite in terms of speech, but they can come across as abrupt, and, as we have seen, are surprisingly impolite when it comes to holding open doors in shops, for example. If you do this, a stream of people may well go through the door without so much as a "thank you!" In speech, however, it is usual to say "thank you" and reply with "you're welcome" ("*palun*"). Note that *palun* also means "please."

BODY LANGUAGE

Estonians are not easy to talk to. If you are unfamiliar with their ways, you may find them unnervingly silent and abrupt. "Russians" may, at a first meeting, come across as much more exuberant and friendly, although Estonians point out that this is no guarantee of loyalty or long-term friendship, and that it may be "false." This is important to remember: Estonians are not generally good at pretense, even when it would be more pleasant for the other person if they were. If they have nothing particularly pleasant to say to you, they are more likely to say nothing. Quite often, however, they are being friendlier than you would suspect, so don't be put off if someone doesn't smile. Foreign employers of locals in service industries have found this difficult to combat: persuading Estonians to smile when it does not come naturally can be challenging.

Physically, Estonians are far from demonstrative. One Englishman, married to an

Estonian and living in Tallinn, expressed his surprise when grandparents greeted their grandchildren by shaking hands. This author, however, greeted her Estonian grandparents in the same way, and never found it strange until it was pointed out to her. It is essential to give personal space to anyone you are talking to and certainly to refrain from touching them, as this could be seen as invasive, offensive, or even overtly flirtatious.

Children are still expected to do a little "bob" when receiving presents. Women often do the same at formal ceremonies.

THESE ARE RUDE!

Most of these are unacceptable behavior else-where too, but it is as well to be forewarned.

- Don't snap your fingers to gain attention, for example in a restaurant.
- Don't yawn in front of someone (at least put your hand to your mouth!).
- Don't point with your forefinger.
- Don't keep your hands in your pockets when you are talking to someone.
- Don't eat with your elbows on the table.
- Don't chew gum close up to someone you are talking to.

On the other hand, there are no rules about whistling, and it is certainly not considered less acceptable for women to whistle than men.

MEDIA
Newspapers and Magazines

For a small country, Estonia has a vibrant press, due in no small part to the editorial freedom that arrived with the restoration of independence. There are five "quality" Estonian-language newspapers (two weekly), as well as two tabloids, and two daily newspapers in Russian. The market is dominated by the tabloid *Ohtuleht* ("Evening Newspaper"), which has a 34 percent market share, and by the broadsheet *Postimees* ("Postman"), at 29 percent; the weekly *Eesti Ekspress* is also popular. There is one daily business paper, the Swedish-owned *Äripäev*. The main English-language newspaper is the weekly *Baltic Times*, which, as the name suggests, also covers Latvia and Lithuania; it is printed in Riga. There is a reasonable selection of English-language newspapers, with the *Financial Times* (printed in Stockholm) available on the day of publication; the *International Herald Tribune* is also widely read. One might expect Russian-language Estonian newspapers to be less biased than Moscow ones, although this is not always the case. The Russian-language radio service, which is Estonian state-run, is more likely to offer fair reports of what is going on in the country.

The market also sustains a number of magazines of both general and specialist interest, the most popular being the gossipy *Kroonika*; more highbrow offerings include *Sirp*, a weekly arts magazine. There are two bimonthly English-language magazines with a focus on Tallinn: *In Your Pocket*, aimed primarily at tourists, with good hotel, restaurant, and nightlife listings, as well as sights and practical information (*IYP* also publishes less frequent guides to Tartu and Parnu); and *The City Paper*, which offers similar listings for Tallinn, Riga, and Vilnius, along with topical features on life, art, and politics in the Baltics. The main source for television listings is the weekly *TV Nädal*.

Broadcast Media

There are three Estonian-language channels: the state-funded ETV and the commercial Kanal 2 and TV3, with the latter pair owned by Norwegian and Swedish companies respectively. Many programs are made by independent companies. There are no Russian-language Estonian channels, but ETV offers daily news broadcasts and weekly shows in Russian; Kanal 2 has Russian-language programs on Sundays.

Those living in northern Estonia also receive the four main Finnish channels; cable gives access to about sixty stations, including Russian and German stations, as well as CNN and BBC World.

The state radio broadcaster, Eesti Raadio, offers four channels: Vikerraadio, with news, documentaries, "self-education" programs and music by Estonian artists; Raadio 2, aimed at younger listeners; Klaasikaraadio, an all-classical channel; and the Russian-language Raadio 4, with news, music, political analysis, and information on employment and legal issues. Eesti Raadio also runs Raadio Tallinn, a service for foreign visitors and residents, with news and features on current affairs in English, French, and German. There are several commercial radio stations, broadcasting in both Estonian and Russian.

The Internet
As you'd expect of a country nicknamed "E-stonia," the Internet has taken off in a big way, with more than half the Estonian population using the Internet regularly—above the EU average— and broadband connection higher than the average in the fifteen "western" EU member states. The Estonian government conducts all its business on computers, and citizens can vote online; most Web sites offer information in English and Russian. Estonian IT know-how contributed to the creation of Skype and Kazaa!, and the country has an excellent Wi-Fi network, with terminals available in most towns and even in remoter areas. Useful Web sites for foreigners in Estonia include expatsinestonia.com, www.expat blog.com/en/ directory/eastern-europe/estonia, and, for cultural, social, and historical information, www.einst.ee and www.estonica.org.

SERVICES
Mail

Post offices are usually open from 9:00 a.m. to 6.00 p.m. on weekdays and 9:30 a.m. to 3:00 p.m. on Saturdays; central post offices in the cities are open later. Domestic post can be delivered within one day, but mail to other countries can be slow, especially beyond the Baltic States. Stamps are sold only at post offices.

Street numbers follow the street name in addresses. The following abbreviations are common: "*tn*" for *täna* (street) and "*mnt*" for *maantee* (avenue or larger street). With very well-known names, for example in the Old Town, it is common to use only the street name, for example "Pikk 40," instead of "Pikk *tn* 40."

Telephone

Telephone services were privatized in 2001, under the terms of a 1992 agreement between the Estonian government and Eesti Telefon, under which the latter agreed to modernize the outdated Soviet network in exchange for its monopoly. However, while there are now rival providers, most use the network established by Eesti Telefon, now called Elion (www.elion.ee). Public telephones work on a phone-card system and do not take cash. Cards can be picked up at vending kiosks and can be used for international calls. The Ekspress hotline is an English-language telephone service offering practical information on a host of topics such as weather, what's on, etc. Call 1182 or visit www.1182.ee.

Estonia is part of the GSM cell-phone network, which operates in most of Western Europe. Estonians love cell phones—you are far more likely to reach them on a mobile number than on a landline—and use them to pay for parking tickets, public transportation, and many other things. International call rates are expensive, and if you are staying in a hotel it may well be cheaper to use the hotel phone when calling abroad.

There are two main telephone directories in Estonia: Infopluss (www.infopluss.ee), for residential numbers and businesses; and Eesti Ettevotted (www.ee.ee), the Estonian Yellow Pages. The latter offers information only in Estonian and Russian. For general directory inquiries, call 1182. Most Estonians, however, do such inquiring online and one of the most popular addresses for this is www.delfi.ee (available in Estonian and Russian).

Answering the Telephone

When answering the telephone in a work context, it is customary to say the name of the office or business, then just "Good morning," or "Good afternoon." Some businesses have imported the addition of "How can I help you?" which some Estonians find rather annoying as they like to get to the point. On a cell phone it is common to answer by saying your first name, followed by "Hello." When answering private landlines, people generally simply answer with a "Hello."

CONCLUSION

Today's Estonia is a young state. Things have calmed down a little since the heady days of the early 1990s, but Estonia is still evolving almost daily. As a result, this book deals necessarily in generalizations, giving a broad rule and a guide that is generally applicable. You may find exceptions to every "rule" mentioned here, or discover that the culture has simply moved on. The stagnation of the Soviet era led born-again Estonia to embrace globalized communications and Western values with unbridled enthusiasm. In the main, however, this remains a country very different from its Nordic and Eastern neighbors, let alone the rest of Europe. Estonians exhibit a peculiar mixture of introspection, modesty, and quiet self-confidence. They have an acute sense of irony and make loyal friends, but to earn their trust, you need to persevere.

Estonia is a land of contrasts, its crowded, cosmopolitan capital seemingly at odds with the empty countryside and the simple rural lifestyle. In its language as well as its culture, it has borrowed the best of the nations that have occupied or traded with it, while retaining its own fiercely guarded traditions and heritage. It takes a while to get to know them, but Estonians are living proof that silence can be golden.

Further Reading

Apart from the readily available English-language tourist guides, the following may be of particular interest.

Agar, Augustus. *Baltic Episode.* London: Hodder and Stougton, 1963.

Dovlatov, Sergei. *Compromise.* New York: Knopf, 1983.

Hillier, Paul. *Arvo Pärt.* Oxford: Oxford University Press, 1997.

Kaplinski, Jaan. *The Same Sea in us All.* London: Harvill, 1990.

———. *The Wandering Border.* London: Harvill, 1992.

———. *Through the Forest.* London: Harvill, 1996.

Kross, Jaan. *The Conspiracy and Other Stories.* London: Harvill, 1992.

———. *Professor Martin's Departure.* London: HarperCollins, 1994.

———. *Treading Air.* London: Harvill, 2003.

Lieven, Anatol. *The Baltic Revolution.* Yale University Press, 1993.

Moseley, Christopher. *From Baltic Shores.* Surrey: Norvkik Press, 1994.

———. *Colloquial Estonian: A Complete Language Course.* London: Routledge, 1994.

Õnnepalu, Tõnu. *Border State.* Illinois: Northwestern University Press, 2000.

Palmer, William, *The Good Republic.* London: Secker & Warburg, 1990.

Ross, Alan, *The Winter Sea.* London: Harvill, 1997.

Seth, Ronald. *Baltic Corner: Travels in Estonia.* London: Methuen, 1938.

Thomson, Clare. *The Singing Revolution.* London: Michael Joseph, 1992.

———. *Tallinn.* Bath: Footprint, 2006.

Unt, Mati. *The Autumn Ball.* Tallinn: Perioodika, 1985.

Index

Acknowledgments

Thank you to Kay Bischoff, Ulvi Haagensen, Anne Härmaste, Vaike Kiik,
Ülle Leis, Marianne and Madis Mikko, Birgit Naur, Tiina Randviir and the
Estonian Institute, Reet Remmel, Paul Rodgers, Heigo Sahk, Andrus
Salupere, Liina Siib, Hille Tamkivi, Paul Taylor, Piret Viires, and the
Estonian Writers' Union.